सीताराम

sundarakāṇḍa
Legacy Book
-
Endowment of Devotion

:

Embellish it with Your
Rama Namas
& Present it to Someone You Love

::

सुन्दरकाण्ड व राम-नाम माला

Belongs to ______________________

Presented to ______________________

____

____

Published by: RAMA-Nama Journals
(an Imprint of e1i1 Corporation)

Title: Sundara-Kanda Legacy Book - Endowment of Devotion
Sub-Title: Embellish it with your Rama Namas & present it to someone you love

Author/Designer: Subhash Chandra

Parts of this book have been derived/inspired from our other publication:
"Sundarakanda The Fifth-Ascent of Tulsi Ramayana" (Authored by Subhash Chandra)

Identifiers

ISBN: **978-1-945739-90-3** (Paperback)
ISBN: **978-1-945739-91-0** (Hardcover)

—o—

⌘⌘⌘⌘⌘⌘⌘⌘⌘⌘⌘⌘⌘⌘⌘⌘⌘⌘⌘⌘⌘⌘⌘⌘⌘⌘⌘⌘⌘
⌘⌘⌘⌘⌘⌘⌘⌘⌘⌘⌘⌘⌘⌘⌘⌘⌘⌘⌘⌘⌘⌘⌘⌘⌘⌘⌘⌘⌘

कलिजुग केवल हरि गुन गाहा । गावत नर पावहिं भव थाहा ॥

kalijuga kevala hari guna gāhā, gāvata nara pāvahiṁ bhava thāhā.

कलिजुग जोग न जग्य न ग्याना । एक अधार राम गुन गाना ॥

kalijuga joga na jagya na gyānā, eka adhāra rāma guna gānā.

The only appointed means for the Kali-Yuga is singing the praises of the Lord—just following that simple path people are able to cross this turbulent worldly life. In this Yuga neither Yoga nor Yagya nor Wisdom is of much avail—the only hope is in chanting the Holy-Name राम राम राम.

⌘⌘⌘⌘⌘

In all the four ages; in all times, past, present, or future; in the three spheres of creation—anyone that repeats the name **राम** becomes blessed. The name of Rāma is like the Tree-of-Heaven, and is the centre of all that is good in the world, and whoever meditates upon it verily becomes transformed—even the vile-most turn holy. As Narasingh became manifest to destroy Hiranyākashyap, the enemy of gods, in order to protect Prahlād—so is the Name of Rāma **राम** for the destruction of the wicked and protection of devout.

The chanting of Rāma-Nāma is a direct way to liberation. By repeating the **राम** name—whether in joy or in sadness, in activity or in repose—bliss is diffused all around. According to the Vedas, just as the Sun dispels darkness, the chanting of Rāma-Nāma dispels all the evils and obstacles of life. The Rāma Nāma cures agony and showers the blessings of God; all righteous wishes get fulfilled; jealousy and pride disappear; life becomes imbued with satisfaction and peace; all of life's needs fall in place naturally—just like a miracle of nature guiding nature's forces. You may not always get what you want in the exact same form, but the Rāma-Nāma will sanctify things and bring to you the same needed happiness and bliss in a much more refined and lasting way. Life truly becomes filled with tranquility. With the Rāma-Nāma, an immense sense of inner spiritual wellbeing is experienced apart from a gain of external material happiness.

⌘⌘⌘⌘⌘

राम नाम मनिदीप धरु जीह देहरीं द्वार ।

rāma nāma manidīpa dharu jīha deharīṁ dvāra,

तुलसी भीतर बाहेरहुँ जौं चाहसि उजिआर ॥

tulasī bhītara bāherahuṁ jauṁ cāhasi ujiāra.

O Tulsīdās, place the luminous gem in the shape of the divine name 'Rāma' on the tongue—which is at the threshold, the doorway to the inside—and you will have light both on inside and outside. (i.e. Always chant **राम**, and its radiance will illumine your mind, body, life—all around, everywhere, inside out.)

—⌘⌘⌘⌘⌘⌘⌘⌘⌘⌘—

Rāma Jayam: Journal for writing the Holy-Name राम. Once embellished with your Rāma-Nāmas, this Journal-Book will become a priceless treasure which you can present to your loved ones—an unparalleled gift of love, labor, caring, wishing, and above all—Devotion.

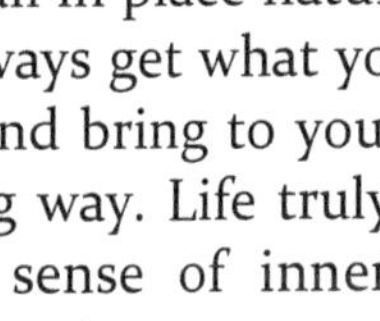

*To write **राम** in Sanskrit, trace the contours 1-2 (which is the sound of **r** in 'run'), 3-4 (the sound **a** in 'ark'), 5-6 & 7-8 (the sound **m** in 'must') and lastly mark the top line 9-10. Please note the pronunciation: **राम** rhymes with calm.*

श्रीराम जयराम जय जय राम
śrīrāma jayarāma jaya jaya rāma

जय जय सीताराम तुलसी
jaya jaya sītārāma tulasī

जय हनुमंते
jaya hanumamte

जय सियाराम सियाराम सिया राम, जय सियाराम सियाराम
jaya siyārāma siyārāma siyā rāma,
jaya siyārāma siyārāma

सीताराम सीताराम सीताराम राम राम,
रामराम रामराम रामराम सीता राम
sītārāma sītārāma sītārāma rāma rāma,
rāmarāma rāmarāma rāmarāma sītā rāma

सियावर रामचंद्र पद जय शरणं सीताराम
siyāvara rāmacamdra pada jaya śaraṇaṁ sitārāma

सियावर राम जय जय राम, मेरे प्रभु राम जय जय राम
siyāvara rāma jaya jaya rāma
mere prabhu rāma jaya jaya rāma

श्री रामः शरणं ममः
śrī rāmaḥ śaraṇaṁ mamaḥ
(I surrender myself & take the shelter of Lord God Shrī Rāma)

मंगल भवन अमंगल हारी ।
द्रवउ सो दसरथ अजिर बिहारी ॥
maṁgala bhavana amaṁgala hārī,
dravau so dasaratha ajira bihārī.
(He who brings auspiciousness and defeats all ills, may [that child] Rāma sporting in Dasrath's court have mercy)

अजर अमर गुननिधि सुत होहू ।
करहुँ बहुत रघुनायक छोहू ॥
ajara amara gunanidhi suta hohū,
karahum̐ bahuta raghunāyaka chohū.
(May you become ageless, deathless, treasury of virtues, and the very blessed of Shrī Rāma, dear)

राजिवनयन धरें धनु सायक ।
भगत बिपति भंजन सुख दायक ॥
rājivanayana dhareṁ dhanu sāyaka,
bhagata bipati bhaṁjana sukha dāyaka.
(Shrī Rāma, our lotus-eyed Lord—who wields bow and arrows—destroys all troubles of devotees and imparts happiness)

जौं प्रभु दीनदयालु कहावा । आरति हरन बेद जसु गावा ॥
jauṁ prabhu dīnadayālu kahāvā,
ārati harana beda jasu gāvā.
(You are the protector of the humble & weak—as the Vedas declare—O Lord, please take away my anguish)

जपहिं नामु जन आरत भारी ।
मिटहिं कुसंकट होहिं सुखारी ॥
japahiṁ nāmu jana ārata bhārī,
miṭahiṁ kusaṁkaṭa hohiṁ sukhārī.
(Afflicted with great distress, we chant your name O Lord; please remove our troubles and grant us felicity)

दीन दयाल बिरिदु संभारी । हरहु नाथ मम संकट भारी ॥
dīna dayāla biridu saṁbhārī,
harahu nātha mama saṁkaṭa bhārī.
(O Lord, you are the protector of weak and the destroyer of obstacles, please remove the great danger that has befallen me)

हनूमान अंगद रन गाजे । हाँक सुनत रजनीचर भाजे ॥
hanūmāna aṁgada rana gāje,
hām̐ka sunata rajanīcara bhāje.
(When Hanumān and Aṁgad roar in the arena, all the wicked/devils run away in fear)

सकल बिघ्न ब्यापहिं नहिं तेही ।
राम सुकृपाँ बिलोकहिं जेही ॥
sakala bighna byāpahiṁ nahiṁ tehī,
rāma sukṛpām̐ bilokahiṁ jehī.
(No troubles ever befall one—upon whom Shrī Rāma bestows His gracious glance)

दैहिक दैविक भौतिक तापा ।
राम राज नहिं काहुहि ब्यापा ॥
daihika daivika bhautika tāpā,
rāma rāja nahiṁ kāhuhi byāpā.
(In the Kingdom of Rāma, there is never any body-given, god-given, man-given afflictions)

प्रबिसि नगर कीजे सब काजा ।
हृदयँ राखि कोसलपुर राजा ॥
prabisi nagara kīje saba kājā,
hṛdayam̐ rākhi kosalapura rājā.
(Enter the city and accomplish all tasks, keeping the King of Kaushal, Shrī Rāma, enshrined within your heart)

जब तें रामु ब्याहि घर आए । नित नव मंगल मोद बधाए ॥
jaba teṁ rāmu byāhi ghara āe,
nita nava maṁgala moda badhāe.
(Ever since Rāma returned home after wedding, there were new festivities every day, all around)

जनकसुता जग जननि जानकी ।
अतिसय प्रिय करुना निधान की ॥
janakasutā jaga janani jānakī,
atisaya priya karunā nidhāna kī.
(I invoke the favor of Jānakī, daughter of Janak, mother of the world, the most beloved of the All-merciful Rāma)

⌘⌘⌘⌘⌘⌘⌘⌘⌘⌘⌘⌘⌘⌘⌘⌘⌘⌘⌘⌘⌘⌘⌘⌘⌘⌘⌘⌘⌘⌘

[मान्यतानुसार सुन्दरकाण्ड पाठ, भगवत्स्मरण पश्चात, किष्किन्धाकाण्ड दोहा २९ से आरम्भ होता है]

[Traditionally, Sundarakānda Pātha begins from kiṣkindhākāṇḍa-Dohā 29, after the chanting of Rāma Nāma and invoking Shrī Hanumāna and others gods]

सीताराम सीताराम

ॐ

विघ्नेश्वराय वरदाय सुरप्रियाय लम्बोदराय सकलाय जगत हिताय ।
vighneśvarāya varadāya surapriyāya lambodarāya sakalāya jagata hitāya,
नागाननाय श्रुतियज्ञविभूषिताय गौरीसुताय गणनाथ नमो नमस्ते ॥
nāgānanāya śrutiyajñavibhūṣitāya gaurīsutāya gaṇanātha namo namaste.

(Salutations to Shrī Ganesh)

⌘

आइये हनुमंत विराजिये कथा कहूं मति अनुसार ।
āiye hanumaṁta virājiye kathā kahūṁ mati anusāra,
प्रेम सहित गादी धरूं पधारिये पवन कुमार ॥
prema sahita gādī dharūṁ padhāriye pavana kumāra.

(Invocations to Shrī Hanumān)

⌘

लोकाभिरामं रणरङ्गधीरं राजीवनेत्रं रघुवंशनाथम् ।
lokābhirāmaṁ raṇaraṅgadhīraṁ rājīvanetraṁ raghuvaṁśanātham,
कारुण्यरूपं करुणाकरं तं श्रीरामचन्द्रं शरणं प्रपद्ये ॥
kāruṇyarūpaṁ karuṇākaraṁ taṁ śrīrāmacandraṁ śaraṇaṁ prapadye.
मनोजवं मारुततुल्यवेगं जितेन्द्रियं बुद्धिमतां वरिष्ठम् ।
manojavaṁ mārutatulyavegaṁ jitendriyaṁ buddhimatāṁ variṣṭham,
वातात्मजं वानरयूथमुख्यं श्रीरामदूतं शरणं प्रपद्ये ॥
vātātmajaṁ vānarayūthamukhyaṁ śrīrāmadūtaṁ śaraṇaṁ prapadye.

(Meditation & Surrender to Shrī Rāma & Hanumān)

⌘

गुरु ब्रह्मा गुरुर्विष्णुः गुरुदेव महेश्वरः ।
guru brahmā gururviṣṇu gurudeva maheśvara,
गुरु साक्षात्परब्रह्म तस्मैश्री गुरुवे नमः ॥
guru sākṣātparabrahma tasmaiśrī guruve namaḥ.

(Salutations to Guru)

⌘

श्रीरामचंद्र भगवान की जय ॥
śrī rāmacaṁdra bhagavāna kī jaya.
पवनसुत हनुमान की जय ॥
pavanasuta hanumāna kī jaya.
गोस्वामी तुलसीदास की जय ॥
gosvāmī tulasīdāsa kī jaya.
ॐ नमः पार्वती पतये हर हर महादेव ॥
OM namaḥ pārvatī pataye hara hara mahādeva.

⌘

श्रीराम जयराम जय जय राम । जयजय राम जयजय राम ॥
śrīrāma jayarāma jaya jaya rāma, jayajaya rāma jayajaya rāma.
श्रीराम जयराम जय जय राम । जयजय राम जयजय राम ॥
śrīrāma jayarāma jaya jaya rāma, jayajaya rāma jayajaya rāma…
…

हरे रामा रामा राम । सीताराम राम राम ॥
hare rāmā rāmā rāma, sītārāma rāma rāma.
हरे रामा रामा राम । सीताराम राम राम ॥
hare rāmā rāmā rāma, sītārāma rāma rāma...
…

⌘

ॐ श्री परमात्मने नमः
OM śrī paramātmane namaḥ

⌘

प्रनवउँ पवनकुमार खल बन पावक ग्यानधन ।
pranavauṁ pavanakumāra khala bana pāvaka gyānadhana,
जासु हृदय आगार बसहिं राम सर चाप धर ॥
jāsu hṛdaya āgāra basahiṁ rāma sara cāpa dhara.
(Obeisance to Shrī Hanumān)

⌘

किष्किन्धाकाण्ड - kiṣkindhākāṇḍa

दोहा-dohā:

बलि बाँधत प्रभु बाढ़ेउ सो तनु बरनि न जाइ ।
bali bāṁdhata prabhu bāṛheu so tanu barani na jāi,
उभय घरी महँ दीन्हीं सात प्रदच्छिन धाइ ॥ २९ ॥
ubhaya gharī mahaṁ dīnhīṁ sāta pradacchina dhāi. 29.

मंगल भवन अमंगल हारी । द्रवउ सो दसरथ अजिर बिहारी ॥
maṁgala bhavana amaṁgala hārī, dravau so dasaratha ajira bihārī.

Trans:

"When he made Valī captive, the Lord grew to an indescribable size; and yet in less than an hour I circumambulated the Lord as many as seven times", [stated Jāmavaṁt.]

चौपाई-caupāī:

अंगद कहइ जाउँ मैं पारा । जियँ संसय कछु फिरती बारा ॥
aṁgada kahai jāuṁ maiṁ pārā, jiyaṁ saṁsaya kachu phiratī bārā.
जामवंत कह तुम्ह सब लायक । पठइअ किमि सब ही कर नायक ॥
jāmavaṁta kaha tumha saba lāyaka, paṭhaia kimi saba hī kara nāyaka.
कहइ रीछपति सुनु हनुमाना । का चुप साधि रहेहु बलवाना ॥
kahai rīkṣapati sunu hanumānā, kā cupa sādhi rahehu balavānā.
पवन तनय बल पवन समाना । बुधि बिबेक बिग्यान निधाना ॥
pavana tanaya bala pavana samānā, budhi bibeka bigyāna nidhānā.

कवन सो काज कठिन जग माहीं । जो नहिं होइ तात तुम्ह पाहीं ॥
kavana so kāja kaṭhina jaga māhīṁ, jo nahiṁ hoi tāta tumha pāhīṁ.
राम काज लगि तव अवतारा । सुनतहिं भयउ पर्बताकारा ॥
rāma kāja lagi tava avatārā, sunatahiṁ bhayau parbatākārā.
कनक बरन तन तेज बिराजा । मानहुँ अपर गिरिन्ह कर राजा ॥
kanaka barana tana teja birājā, mānahuṁ apara girinha kara rājā.
सिंहनाद करि बारहिं बारा । लीलहिं नाघउँ जलनिधि खारा ॥
siṁhanāda kari bārahiṁ bārā, līlahiṁ nāghauṁ jalanidhi khārā.
सहित सहाय रावनहि मारी । आनउँ इहाँ त्रिकूट उपारी ॥
sahita sahāya rāvanahi mārī, ānauṁ ihāṁ trikūṭa upārī.
जामवंत मैं पूँछउँ तोही । उचित सिखावनु दीजहु मोही ॥
jāmavaṁta maiṁ pūṁchauṁ tohī, ucita sikhāvanu dījahu mohī.
एतना करहु तात तुम्ह जाई । सीतहि देखि कहहु सुधि आई ॥
etanā karahu tāta tumha jāī, sītahi dekhi kahahu sudhi āī.
तब निज भुज बल राजिवनैना । कौतुक लागि संग कपि सेना ॥
taba nija bhuja bala rājivanainā, kautuka lāgi saṁga kapi senā.

Trans:

Aṁgad said, "I can leap across to the other side but have doubts in my heart about coming back." Jāmavaṁt replied, "You are quite competent but what need there is to send our very chief? Now listen Hanumān, why are you, our mighty champion, so silent? Son of the wind-god, strong as your Sire, you are a veritable mine of intelligence, prudence and wisdom. In all the worlds which undertaking is there so hard that you cannot accomplish it, son? Verily it is only to perform the work of Shrī Rāma that you have taken advent upon earth." Hearing this Hanumān—with a body of golden hue and dazzling splendor—swelled to the size of a mountain, the very king of mountains; and roaring again and again like a bellicose lion, he thundered, "I will step across this salty stream in a mere play. Slaying Rāvan and his enforcements, I will uproot the mount Trikūt and bring it right here. Now I ask you, Jāmavaṁt—just instruct me what ought I to do?—suggest to me the proper course" "Only do this much dear: go see Sītā and return with glad tidings of her; verily our lotus-eyed Lord will then Himself recover Sītā by the might of his arms—taking with him the monkey hosts merely for sport.

छंद-chaṁda:

कपि सेन संग सँघारि निसिचर रामु सीतहि आनिहैं ।
kapi sena saṁga saṁghāri nisicara rāmu sītahi ānihaiṁ,
त्रैलोक पावन सुजसु सुर मुनि नारदादि बखानिहैं ॥
trailoka pāvana sujasu sura muni nāradādi bakhānihaiṁ.
जो सुनत गावत कहत समुझत परम पद नर पावई ।
jo sunata gāvata kahata samujhata parama pada nara pāvaī,
रघुबीर पद पाथोज मधुकर दास तुलसी गावई ॥
raghubīra pada pāthoja madhukara dāsa tulasī gāvaī.

Trans:

Taking with Him an army of monkeys Shrī Rāma will destroy the demons and bring Sītā back. And the gods and saints and Nārad and others will get to recount the glories of Shrī Rāma which will sanctify the three spheres of creation for all times to come. Hearing, and singing, and telling the glories of our Lord, mankind will ascend to the highest dominion. And Tulsīdās—who is devoted like a bee to the lotus feet of the Hero of Raghu's lineage—will ever get to sing of them.

दोहा-dohā:

भव भेषज रघुनाथ जसु सुनहिं जे नर अरु नारि ।
bhava bheṣaja raghunātha jasu sunahiṁ je nara aru nāri,
तिन्ह कर सकल मनोरथ सिद्ध करहिं त्रिसिरारि ॥ ३०क ॥
tinha kara sakala manoratha siddha karahiṁ trisirāri. 30(ka).

Trans:

Verily He, Raghunāth, the slayer of the demon Trisira, grants all desires of men and women that listen to this glorious saga—which is the assured panacea for all the ills of life.

सोरठा-soraṭhā:

नीलोत्पल तन स्याम काम कोटि सोभा अधिक ।
nīlotpala tana syāma kāma koṭi sobhā adhika,
सुनिअ तासु गुन ग्राम जासु नाम अघ खग बधिक ॥ ३०ख ॥
sunia tāsu guna grāma jāsu nāma agha khaga badhika. 30(kha).

मंगल भवन अमंगल हारी । द्रवउ सो दसरथ अजिर बिहारी ॥
maṁgala bhavana amaṁgala hārī, dravau so dasaratha ajira bihārī.

Trans:

Hearken O world to the glories of Shrī Rāma—with his body dark of hue as a blue lotus, whose beauty surpasses that of million Kāmdevas, whose name is a veritable fowler for birds in the shape of sins.

::—::

सीताराम
सीताराम सीताराम
तारामसीताराम
सीताराम सीताराम

ॐ

सीताराम सीताराम सीताराम
सीताराम सीताराम सीताराम सीताराम सीताराम
सीताराम सीताराम सीताराम सीताराम सीताराम सीताराम

श्रीजानकीवल्लभो विजयते
śrījānakīvallabho vijayate

श्रीरामचरितमानस
śrīrāmacaritamānasa

पञ्चम सोपान - सुन्दरकाण्ड
pañcama sopāna - sundarakāṇḍa

श्लोक-śloka:

शान्तं शाश्वतमप्रमेयमनघं निर्वाणशान्तिप्रदं
śāntaṁ śāśvatamaprameyamanaghaṁ nirvāṇaśāntipradaṁ
ब्रह्माशम्भुफणीन्द्रसेव्यमनिशं वेदान्तवेद्यं विभुम्।
brahmāśambhuphaṇīndrasevyamaniśaṁ vedāntavedyaṁ vibhum,
रामाख्यं जगदीश्वरं सुरगुरुं मायामनुष्यं हरिं
rāmākhyaṁ jagadīśvaraṁ suraguruṁ māyāmanuṣyaṁ hariṁ
वन्देऽहं करुणाकरं रघुवरं भूपालचूडामणिम्॥१॥
vande'haṁ karuṇākaraṁ raghuvaraṁ bhūpālacūṛāmaṇim. 1 .

I adore the Lord of the universe—immeasurable, all pervading and eternal, the very theme of Vedanta, beyond ordinary means of cognition, the all-merciful God of gods constantly worshipped by Brahmmā, Shambhu and Shesha; the dispeller of all sins, bestower of the supreme beatitude of emancipation, a veritable mine of compassion, the Lord God Hari appearing through his Māyā in the form of man, the King of kings, the chief of Raghus—Shrī Rāma.

जब तें रामु ब्याहि घर आए। नित नव मंगल मोद बधाए॥
दीन दयाल बिरिदु संभारी। हरहु नाथ मम संकट भारी॥
मंगल भवन अमंगल हारी। द्रवउ सो दसरथ अजिर बिहारी॥

प्रबिसि नगर कीजे सब काजा। हृदयँ राखि कोसलपुर राजा॥
जपहिं नामु जन आरत भारी। मिटहिं कुसंकट होहिं सुखारी॥
सियावर राम जय जय राम। मेरे प्रभु राम जय जय राम॥

Dt: ____________________

नान्या स्पृहा रघुपते हृदयेऽस्मदीये
nānyā spṛhā raghupate hṛdaye'smadīye
सत्यं वदामि च भवानखिलान्तरात्मा ।
satyaṁ vadāmi ca bhavānakhilāntarātmā,
भक्तिं प्रयच्छ रघुपुङ्गव निर्भरां मे
bhaktiṁ prayaccha raghupuṅgava nirbharāṁ me
कामादिदोषरहितं कुरु मानसं च ॥ २ ॥
kāmādidoṣarahitaṁ kuru mānasaṁ ca. 2 .

There is no other craving in my heart, O Lord, and I speak the truth and you know my inmost thoughts—for you are the indwelling Spirit in the hearts of all—do please grant me, O crest-jewel of Raghus, the intense-most devotion to Thy Holy Feet; and make my heart clean of lust and every other sin.

अतुलितबलधामं हेमशैलाभदेहं
atulitabaladhāmaṁ hemaśailābhadehaṁ
दनुजवनकृशानुं ज्ञानिनामग्रगण्यम् ।
danujavanakṛśānuṁ jñānināmagragaṇyam,
सकलगुणनिधानं वानराणामधीशं
sakalaguṇanidhānaṁ vānarāṇāmadhīśaṁ
रघुपतिप्रियभक्तं वातजातं नमामि ॥३॥
raghupatipriyabhaktaṁ vātajātaṁ namāmi. 3 .

Repeatedly I bow to the son-of-wind-god: repository of immeasurable might, with his body shining like a mountain of gold, the very blazing fire that devours the forest in the shape of demons; the abode of virtues, the noblest messenger of Raghupati, foremost amongst the wise, the chief of the monkeys: Shrī Hanumān, the most beloved devotee of Shrī Rāma.

Dt: ______________________

जब तें रामु ब्याहि घर आए । नित नव मंगल मोद बधाए ॥
दीन दयाल बिरिदु संभारी । हरहु नाथ मम संकट भारी ॥
मंगल भवन अमंगल हारी । द्रवउ सो दसरथ अजिर बिहारी ॥

प्रबिसि नगर कीजे सब काजा । हृदयँ राखि कोसलपुर राजा ॥
जपहिं नामु जन आरत भारी । मिटहिं कुसंकट होहिं सुखारी ॥
सियावर राम जय जय राम । मेरे प्रभु राम जय जय राम ॥

चौपाई-*caupāī:*

जामवंत के बचन सुहाए । सुनि हनुमंत हृदय अति भाए ॥
jāmavaṁta ke bacana suhāe, suni hanumaṁta hṛdaya ati bhāe .
तब लगि मोहि परिखेहु तुम्ह भाई । सहि दुख कंद मूल फल खाई ॥
taba lagi mohi parikhehu tumha bhāī, sahi dukha kaṁda mūla phala khāī .
जब लगि आवौं सीतहि देखी । होइहि काजु मोहि हरष बिसेषी ॥
jaba lagi āvauṁ sītahi dekhī, hoihi kāju mohi haraṣa biseṣī .
यह कहि नाइ सबन्हि कहुँ माथा । चलेउ हरषि हियँ धरि रघुनाथा ॥
yaha kahi nāi sabanhi kahum̐ māthā, caleu haraṣi hiyam̐ dhari raghunāthā .
सिंधु तीर एक भूधर सुंदर । कौतुक कूदि चढ़ेउ ता ऊपर ॥
siṁdhu tīra eka bhūdhara suṁdara, kautuka kūdi caṛheu tā ūpara .
बार बार रघुबीर सँभारी । तरकेउ पवनतनय बल भारी ॥
bāra bāra raghubīra sam̐bhārī, tarakeu pavanatanaya bala bhārī .
जेहिं गिरि चरन देइ हनुमंता । चलेउ सो गा पाताल तुरंता ॥
jehiṁ giri carana dei hanumaṁtā, caleu so gā pātāla turaṁtā .
जिमि अमोघ रघुपति कर बाना । एही भाँति चलेउ हनुमाना ॥
jimi amogha raghupati kara bānā, ehī bhām̐ti caleu hanumānā .
जलनिधि रघुपति दूत बिचारी । तैं मैनाक होहि श्रमहारी ॥
jalanidhi raghupati dūta bicārī, taiṁ maināka hohi śramahārī .

Hearing the heartening speech of Jāmavaṁt, Hanumān greatly rejoiced in his heart and said, “Endure these hardships my brothers, and with roots, herbs, fruits as your food, await here my return—till I am back with the news of Mā Sītā. My objective will surely be accomplished—I experience this great exhilaration in my heart.” Saying so he bowed his head to them all; and then, with the image of Shrī Rāma enshrined in his heart, and full of exuberance, Hanumān sallied forth. There was a majestic rock by the seashore and Hanumān sprang upon its top in mere sport.

दोहा-dohā:

हनूमान तेहि परसा कर पुनि कीन्ह प्रनाम ।

hanūmāna tehi parasā kara puni kīnha pranāma,

राम काजु कीन्हें बिनु मोहि कहाँ बिश्राम ॥ १ ॥

rāma kāju kīnheṁ binu mohi kahāṁ biśrāma. 1 .

Then again and again invoking the name of Raghubīr, the son-of-wind leaped with all his might. And the hill upon which he had planted his foot instantly sank—recoiling into the nethermost world. And just like an exceeding unerring arrow fired by Raghupati, Hanumān sped away. On the way—and knowing Hanumān to be the emissary of Shrī Rāma—the deity presiding over the Ocean told Maināk, "Relieve him of his fatigue."

[Mount Maināk raised himself up from the sea and stood before, in welcome,] but Hanumān merely touched it with his hand, and saluting to it said, "There can be no rest for me until I have accomplished the work of Shri Rāma."

जब तें रामु ब्याहि घर आए । नित नव मंगल मोद बधाए ॥
दीन दयाल बिरिदु संभारी । हरहु नाथ मम संकट भारी ॥
मंगल भवन अमंगल हारी । द्रवउ सो दसरथ अजिर बिहारी ॥

प्रबिसि नगर कीजे सब काजा । हृदयँ राखि कोसलपुर राजा ॥
जपहिं नामु जन आरत भारी । मिटहिं कुसंकट होहिं सुखारी ॥
सियावर राम जय राम जय राम । मेरे प्रभु राम जय राम जय राम ॥

चौपाई-caupāī:

जात पवनसुत देवन्ह देखा । जानैं कहुँ बल बुद्धि बिसेषा ॥
jāta pavanasuta devanha dekhā, jānaiṁ kahum̐ bala buddhi biseṣā .
सुरसा नाम अहिन्ह कै माता । पठइन्हि आइ कही तेहिं बाता ॥
surasā nāma ahinha kai mātā, paṭhainhi āi kahī tehiṁ bātā .
आजु सुरन्ह मोहि दीन्ह अहारा । सुनत बचन कह पवनकुमारा ॥
āju suranha mohi dīnha ahārā, sunata bacana kaha pavanakumārā .
राम काजु करि फिरि मैं आवौं । सीता कइ सुधि प्रभुहि सुनावौं ॥
rāma kāju kari phiri maiṁ āvauṁ, sītā kai sudhi prabhuhi sunāvauṁ .
तब तव बदन पैठिहउँ आई । सत्य कहउँ मोहि जान दे माई ॥
taba tava badana paiṭhihaum̐ āī, satya kahaum̐ mohi jāna de māī .
कवनेहुँ जतन देइ नहिं जाना । ग्रससि न मोहि कहेउ हनुमाना ॥
kavanehum̐ jatana dei nahiṁ jānā, grasasi na mohi kaheu hanumānā .
जोजन भरि तेहिं बदनु पसारा । कपि तनु कीन्ह दुगुन बिस्तारा ॥
jojana bhari tehiṁ badanu pasārā, kapi tanu kīnha duguna bistārā .
सोरह जोजन मुख तेहिं ठयऊ । तुरत पवनसुत बत्तिस भयऊ ॥
soraha jojana mukha tehiṁ ṭhayaū, turata pavanasuta battisa bhayaū .
जस जस सुरसा बदनु बढ़ावा । तासु दून कपि रूप देखावा ॥
jasa jasa surasā badanu baṛhāvā, tāsu dūna kapi rūpa dekhāvā .
सत जोजन तेहिं आनन कीन्हा । अति लघु रूप पवनसुत लीन्हा ॥
sata jojana tehiṁ ānana kīnhā, ati laghu rūpa pavanasuta līnhā .
बदन पइठि पुनि बाहेर आवा । मागा बिदा ताहि सिरु नावा ॥
badana paiṭhi puni bāhera āvā, māgā bidā tāhi siru nāvā .
मोहि सुरन्ह जेहि लागि पठावा । बुधि बल मरमु तोर मै पावा ॥
mohi suranha jehi lāgi paṭhāvā, budhi bala maramu tora mai pāvā .

When the gods saw the son-of-wind speeding along—and in order to make a trial of his exceptional strength and intellect—they dispatched Sursā, the mother of serpents. She came near Hanumān, as if to devour him, and hollered, "Thank heavens, for the gods have sent me a meal today!" Hearing that, the son-of-wind spoke, "After I have accomplished Rāma's task and have given the news of Shri Sītā to Rāma, then I, of my own accord, will enter thy mouth—truly I tell thee O mother; for now just let me go." But Sursā didn't relent and wouldn't allow Hanumān to get past her by any means; whereupon he said, "Go ahead, devour me then."

जब तें रामु ब्याहि घर आए । नित नव मंगल मोद बधाए ॥
दीन दयाल बिरिदु संभारी । हरहु नाथ मम संकट भारी ॥
मंगल भवन अमंगल हारी । द्रवउ सो दसरथ अजिर बिहारी ॥

दोहा-*dohā:*

राम काजु सबु करिहहु तुम्ह बल बुद्धि निधान ।
rāma kāju sabu karihahu tumha bala buddhi nidhāna,
आसिष देह गई सो हरषि चलेउ हनुमान ॥ २ ॥
āsiṣa deha gaī so harasi caleu hanumāna. 2

प्रबिसि नगर कीजे सब काजा । हृदयँ राखि कोसलपुर राजा ॥
जपहिं नामु जन आरत भारी । मिटहिं कुसंकट होहिं सुखारी ॥
सियावर राम जय जय राम । मेरे प्रभु राम जय जय राम ॥

She opened her jaws a league wide; and the monkey made himself twice as large. She stretched her mouth a sixteen league, and Hanumān at once becomes thirty-two. However large Sursā distended her jaws, the monkey made himself twice as large again. When she had extended her jaws a hundred leagues, Hanumān immediately reduced himself to a tiny size; then, entering her mouth, he came outright back again; and bowing he stood before her, asking permission to leave. "Verily I have gauged the extent of your wit and strength—the errand upon which the gods to me had sent.
You will assuredly accomplish Rāma's work—a storehouse that you are of strength and sagacity." Having thusly blessed him, she retreated. And Hanumān joyfully sped along on his way.

Dt: ______________________

चौपाई-*caupāī:*

निसिचरि एक सिंधु महुँ रहई । करि माया नभु के खग गहई ॥
nisicari eka siṁdhu mahuṁ rahaī, kari māyā nabhu ke khaga gahaī .
जीव जंतु जे गगन उड़ाहीं । जल बिलोकि तिन्ह कै परिछाहीं ॥
jīva jaṁtu je gagana uṛāhīṁ, jala biloki tinha kai parichāhīṁ .
गहइ छाहँ सक सो न उड़ाई । एहि बिधि सदा गगनचर खाई ॥
gahai chāhaṁ saka so na uṛāī, ehi bidhi sadā gaganacara khāī .
सोइ छल हनूमान कहँ कीन्हा । तासु कपटु कपि तुरतहिं चीन्हा ॥
soi chala hanūmāna kahaṁ kīnhā, tāsu kapaṭu kapi turatahiṁ cīnhā .
ताहि मारि मारुतसुत बीरा । बारिधि पार गयउ मतिधीरा ॥
tāhi māri mārutasuta bīrā, bāridhi pāra gayau matidhīrā .

Now in the ocean there dwelt a she-monster who would eat birds from the sky by conjuring wizardry. Beings coursing through air cast shadow upon water and she was able to catch that shadow in such a way that they became ensnared. This way she devoured many flying beings who flew that way—and today she contrived to play the same trick upon Hanumān. But Hanumān at once saw through her craftiness and—resolute of mind, that valiant son-of-wind—forthwith slew the monster. Then joyfully he coursed along on his way till he reached the other shore.

जब तें रामु ब्याहि घर आए । नित नव मंगल मोद बधाए ॥
दीन दयाल बिरिदु संभारी । हरहु नाथ मम संकट भारी ॥
मंगल भवन अमंगल हारी । द्रवउ सो दसरथ अजिर बिहारी ॥

तहाँ जाइ देखी बन सोभा । गुंजत चंचरीक मधु लोभा ॥
tahām̐ jāi dekhī bana sobhā, guṁjata caṁcarīka madhu lobhā :
नाना तरु फल फूल सुहाए । खग मृग बृंद देखि मन भाए ॥
nānā taru phala phūla suhāe, khaga mṛga bṛṁda dekhi mana bhāe .
सैल बिसाल देखि एक आगें । ता पर धाइ चढेउ भय त्यागें ॥
saila bisāla dekhi eka āgeṁ, tā para dhāi caḍheu bhaya tyāgeṁ .
उमा न कछु कपि कै अधिकाई । प्रभु प्रताप जो कालहि खाई ॥
umā na kachu kapi kai adhikāī, prabhu pratāpa jo kālahi khāī .
गिरि पर चढि लंका तेहिं देखी । कहि न जाइ अति दुर्ग बिसेषी ॥
giri para caḍhi laṁkā tehiṁ dekhī, kahi na jāi ati durga biseṣī :
अति उतंग जलनिधि चहु पासा । कनक कोट कर परम प्रकासा ॥
ati utaṁga jalanidhi cahu pāsā, kanaka koṭa kara parama prakāsā .

प्रबिसि नगर कीजे सब काजा । हृदयँ राखि कोसलपुर राजा ॥
जपहिं नामु जन आरत भारी । मिटहिं कुसंकट होहिं सुखारी ॥
सियावर राम जय जय राम । मेरे प्रभु राम जय जय राम ॥

Arriving there Hanumān found himself in a forest quite pleasant to behold—full of diverse trees all resplendent, replete with fruits and flowers, and with swarms of bees humming in quest of nectar, and with multitudes of birds and deer—a most lovely sight to delight the eyes. Seeing a large hillock ahead Hanumān fearlessly sprang upon its top. [And so, from one rock on yon shore to this one here, across a vast ocean, miraculously Hanumān had arrived!] But know, O Umā [said Shiva], all this was not by dint of the monkey's might, but t'was all by the grace of the Lord-God—He who can devour even Death himself [what then to say of these little impediments]. From that summit Hanumān surveyed the city of Lankā: a magnificent fortress that defied description—with its many ramparts of gold shedding a dazzling splendor all around and surrounded by deep seas on all the four sides.

Dt: ____________________

छंद-*chaṁda:*

कनक कोट बिचित्र मनि कृत सुंदरायतना घना ।
kanaka koṭa bicitra mani kṛta suṁdarāyatanā ghanā,
चउहट्ट हट्ट सुबट्ट बीथीं चारु पुर बहु बिधि बना ॥
cauhaṭṭa haṭṭa subaṭṭa bīthīṁ cāru pura bahu bidhi banā.
गज बाजि खच्चर निकर पदचर रथ बरूथन्हि को गनै ।
gaja bāji khaccara nikara padacara ratha barūthanhi ko ganai.
बहुरूप निसिचर जूथ अतिबल सेन बरनत नहिं बनै ॥ १ ॥
bahurūpa nisicara jūtha atibala sena baranata nahiṁ banai. 1.

The charming city was enclosed by fortification walls made of gold and studded with wonderful gems of every type. The city, well decorated in every which way—with magnificent highways, lanes, cross roads, bazaars, and beautiful houses—was a marvelous sight to behold. Who could count the multitudes of horses, mules & elephants, arrays of footmen & chariots, and troops of demons of different builds and shapes—a formidable host that defied every description?

बन बाग उपबन बाटिका सर कूप बापीं सोहहीं ।
bana bāga upabana bāṭikā sara kūpa bāpīṁ sohahīṁ,
नर नाग सुर गंधर्ब कन्या रूप मुनि मन मोहहीं ॥
nara nāga sura gaṁdharba kanyā rūpa muni mana mohahīṁ .
कहुँ माल देह बिसाल सैल समान अतिबल गर्जहीं ।
kahuṁ māla deha bisāla saila samāna atibala garjahīṁ,
नाना अखारेन्ह भिरहिं बहु बिधि एक एकन्ह तर्जहीं ॥२॥
nānā akhārenha bhirahiṁ bahu bidhi eka ekanha tarjahīṁ. 2 .

Groves and orchards, gardens and pastures, woods, ponds, wells and lakes, large and small, all shone lovely and resplendent. And at the sight of fair damsels there—of human descent and Nāgas, and of gods and Gandharvas—the soul of even a hermit would be ravished. And here thundered mighty wrestlers of monstrous forms, grappling each other in various duels in different courts;

करि जतन भट कोटिन्ह बिकट तन नगर चहुँ दिसि रच्छहीं ।
kari jatana bhaṭa koṭinha bikaṭa tana nagara cahum̐ disi racchahīṁ,
कहुँ महिष मानषु धेनु खर अज खल निसाचर भच्छहीं ॥
kahum̐ mahiṣa mānaṣu dhenu khara aja khala nisācara bhacchahīṁ.
एहि लागि तुलसीदास इन्ह की कथा कछु एक है कही ।
ehi lāgi tulasīdāsa inha kī kathā kachu eka hai kahī,
रघुबीर सर तीरथ सरीरन्हि त्यागि गति पैहहिं सही ॥३॥
raghubīra sara tīratha sarīranhi tyāgi gati paihahiṁ sahī. 3 .

and there teemed myriad warriors of frightful forms, sedulously guarding the city on all its four sides. Elsewhere horrid demons were seen banqueting on buffaloes, humans, oxen, donkeys, goats. They would eventually lose their lives to Rāma's hallowed shafts and enter His Divine Abode—and it is for this reason that Tulsīdās gives a few words of mention to them here.

दोहा-*dohā:*

पुर रखवारे देखि बहु कपि मन कीन्ह बिचार ।
pura rakhavāre dekhi bahu kapi mana kīnha bicāra,
अति लघु रूप धरौं निसि नगर करौं पइसार ॥ ३ ॥
ati laghu rūpa dharauṁ nisi nagara karauṁ paisāra. 3 .

Seeing an abundance of city guards, the monkey thought to himself, 'I must make myself very small and slip into the city by night.'

चौपाई-*caupāī:*

मसक समान रूप कपि धरी । लंकहि चलेउ सुमिरि नरहरी ॥
masaka samāna rūpa kapi dharī, laṁkahi caleu sumiri naraharī .
नाम लंकिनी एक निसिचरी । सो कह चलेसि मोहि निंदरी ॥
nāma laṁkinī eka nisicarī, so kaha calesi mohi niṁdarī .
जानेहि नहीं मरमु सठ मोरा । मोर अहार जहाँ लगि चोरा ॥
jānehi nahīṁ maramu saṭha morā, mora ahāra jahām̐ lagi corā .
मुठिका एक महा कपि हनी । रुधिर बमत धरनीं ढनमनी ॥
muṭhikā eka mahā kapi hanī, rudhira bamata dharanīṁ ḍhanamanī .
पुनि संभारि उठि सो लंका । जोरि पानि कर बिनय संसका ॥
puni saṁbhāri uṭhi so laṁkā, jori pāni kara binaya saṁsakā .
जब रावनहि ब्रह्म बर दीन्हा । चलत बिरंचि कहा मोहि चीन्हा ॥
jaba rāvanahi brahma bara dīnhā, calata biraṁci kahā mohi cīnhā .
बिकल होसि तैं कपि कें मारे । तब जानेसु निसिचर संघारे ॥
bikala hosi taiṁ kapi keṁ māre, taba jānesu nisicara saṁghāre .
तात मोर अति पुन्य बहूता । देखेउँ नयन राम कर दूता ॥
tāta mora ati punya bahūtā, dekheum̐ nayana rāma kara dūtā .

When the time came, Hanumān assumed a form tiny as a gnat and entered Lankā invoking the name of the Lord-God. At the gate a she-monster, by the name Lankini, accosted him, "How dare you enter here in contempt of me? O fool, know you not of me? Every thief hereabout is my prey?" Whereupon the monkey dealt her a blow with his fist—and she toppled down, spewing blood from her mouth. Then recovering she stood up in dismay, and with clasped hands made this humble submission: "When Brahma granted Rāvan the boon he sought, he also gave me this clue while departing: 'When worsted by a monkey, know then that it will soon be over with the demon race.' My meritorious deeds, O dear, must have been many and great—for today I have been rewarded by the very sight of Rāma's emissary.

जब तें रामु ब्याहि घर आए । नित नव मंगल मोद बधाए ॥
दीन दयाल बिरिदु संभारी । हरहु नाथ मम संकट भारी ॥
मंगल भवन अमंगल हारी । द्रवउ सो दसरथ अजिर बिहारी ॥

दोहा-*dohā:*

तात स्वर्ग अपबर्ग सुख धरिअ तुला एक अंग ।
tāta svarga apabarga sukha dharia tulā eka aṁga,
तूल न ताहि सकल मिलि जो सुख लव सतसंग ॥४॥
tūla na tāhi sakala mili jo sukha lava satasaṁga. 4 .

प्रबिसि नगर कीजे सब काजा । हृदयँ राखि कोसलपुर राजा ॥
जपहिं नामु जन आरत भारी । मिटहिं कुसंकट होहिं सुखारी ॥
सियावर राम जय जय राम । मेरे प्रभु राम जय जय राम ॥

Listen O dear: on one side of the scale put together all the delights of heavens—as also the bliss of final emancipation—but still they are easily outweighed by just a fraction of joy which results from communion with the saints.

Dt: ____________________

चौपाई-*caupāī:*

प्रबिसि नगर कीजे सब काजा । हृदयँ राखि कोसलपुर राजा ॥
prabisi nagara kīje saba kājā, hṛdayaṁ rākhi kosalapura rājā .
गरल सुधा रिपु करहिं मिताई । गोपद सिंधु अनल सितलाई ॥
garala sudhā ripu karahiṁ mitāī, gopada siṁdhu anala sitalāī .
गरुड़ सुमेरु रेनु सम ताही । राम कृपा करि चितवा जाही ॥
garuṛa sumeru renu sama tāhī, rāma kṛpā kari citavā jāhī .
अति लघु रूप धरेउ हनुमाना । पैठा नगर सुमिरि भगवाना ॥
ati laghu rūpa dhareu hanumānā, paiṭhā nagara sumiri bhagavānā .
मंदिर मंदिर प्रति करि सोधा । देखे जहँ तहँ अगनित जोधा ॥
maṁdira maṁdira prati kari sodhā, dekhe jahaṁ tahaṁ aganita jodhā .
गयउ दसानन मंदिर माहीं । अति बिचित्र कहि जात सो नाहीं ॥
gayau dasānana maṁdira māhīṁ, ati bicitra kahi jāta so nāhīṁ .
सयन किएँ देखा कपि तेही । मंदिर महुँ न दीखि बैदेही ॥
sayana kieṁ dekhā kapi tehī, maṁdira mahuṁ na dīkhi baidehī .
भवन एक पुनि दीख सुहावा । हरि मंदिर तहँ भिन्न बनावा ॥
bhavana eka puni dīkha suhāvā, hari maṁdira tahaṁ bhinna banāvā .

Now, with the Lord of Kaushal enshrined in your heart, go enter the city and accomplish your task." Verily deadly poison becomes ambrosia; and foe turns into friend; and ocean becomes as like water collected in a tiny hoof-print; and fire becomes tranquil chill; and Mount Meru appears like a grain of sand, O Garuda [said Bhushundi], for such a one upon whom Shrī Rāma has cast his gracious glance! And so in the tiny form which he had assumed, Hanumān entered the city invoking the name of Shrī Rāma. Carefully inspecting every separate quarter he combed his way through many mansions and saw countless warriors who dwelt there. When he came upon Rāvan's palace its magnificence was past all telling. Hanumān saw the demon king buried deep in sleep but could find no signs of Videha's daughter anywhere. Hanumān then noticed another splendid building nearby which stood very distinct—with the holy temple of Lord Hari set apart.

जब तें रामु ब्याहि घर आए । नित नव मंगल मोद बधाए ॥
दीन दयाल बिरिदु संभारी । हरहु नाथ मम संकट भारी ॥
मंगल भवन अमंगल हारी । द्रवउ सो दसरथ अजिर बिहारी ॥

दोहा-doha:

रामायुध अंकित गृह सोभा बरनि न जाइ ।
rāmāyudha aṁkita gṛha sobhā barani na jāi,
नव तुलसिका बृंद तहँ देखि हरष कपिराइ ॥५॥
nava tulasikā bṛṁda tahaṁ dekhi harasa kapirāi. 5 .

प्रबिसि नगर कीजे सब काजा । हृदयँ राखि कोसलपुर राजा ॥
जपहिं नामु जन आरत भारी । मिटहिं कुसंकट होहिं सुखारी ॥
सियावर राम जय जय राम । मेरे प्रभु राम जय जय राम ॥

That home, too beautiful to describe, was embellished with bow and arrows—weapons of Shrī Rāma, that indescribable charm—emblazoned upon its walls; and with clusters of young Tulsi plants all around. The monkey chief rejoiced to see such auspicious signs.

Dt: ______________________

चौपाई-*caupāī:*

लंका निसिचर निकर निवासा । इहाँ कहाँ सज्जन कर बासा ॥
lamkā nisicara nikara nivāsā, ihāṁ kahāṁ sajjana kara bāsā .
मन महुँ तरक करैं कपि लागा । तेहीं समय बिभीषनु जागा ॥
mana mahuṁ taraka karaiṁ kapi lāgā, tehīṁ samaya bibhīṣanu jāgā .
राम राम तेहिं सुमिरन कीन्हा । हृदयँ हरष कपि सज्जन चीन्हा ॥
rāma rāma tehiṁ sumirana kīnhā, hṛdayaṁ haraṣa kapi sajjana cīnhā .
एहि सन हठि करिहउँ पहिचानी । साधु ते होइ न कारज हानी ॥
ehi sana haṭhi karihauṁ pahicānī, sādhu te hoi na kāraja hānī .
बिप्र रुप धरि बचन सुनाए । सुनत बिभीषन उठि तहँ आए ॥
bipra rupa dhari bacana sunāe, sunata bibhīṣana uṭhi tahaṁ āe .
करि प्रनाम पूँछी कुसलाई । बिप्र कहहु निज कथा बुझाई ॥
kari pranāma pūṁchī kusalāī, bipra kahahu nija kathā bujhāī .
की तुम्ह हरि दासन्ह महँ कोई । मोरें हृदय प्रीति अति होई ॥
kī tumha hari dāsanha mahaṁ koī, moreṁ hṛdaya prīti ati hoī .
की तुम्ह रामु दीन अनुरागी । आयहु मोहि करन बड़भागी ॥
kī tumha rāmu dīna anurāgī, āyahu mohi karana baṛabhāgī .

"Lankā is the abode of gangs of demons—so how then can a pious soul have his home here?" While the monkey was thus reasoning to himself the owner Vibhishan awoke and, as was his wont, began to chant the Holy Name 'Rāma'. Hanumān became extremely delighted having spied a virtuous soul. 'I shall perforce get to know him at once—for, from a saintly man, no harm can ensue to one's good cause.' Having thus resolved, Hanumān assumed the form of a Brahmin and hailed Vibhishan. Hearing being called, Vibhishan stepped forward and greeted him and asked of his welfare: "Tell me O reverend, who may you be? Are you one of Shrī Hari's very own servants?—for my heart is filled with such exceeding joy at your very sight. Or are you sir Shrī Rāma Himself—the loving supplicant of the poor, come arrived to bless me with His holy sight?

जब तें रामु ब्याहि घर आए । नित नव मंगल मोद बधाए ॥
दीन दयाल बिरिदु संभारी । हरहु नाथ मम संकट भारी ॥
मंगल भवन अमंगल हारी । द्रवउ सो दसरथ अजिर बिहारी ॥

दोहा-dohā:

तब हनुमंत कही सब राम कथा निज नाम ।

taba hanumaṁta kahī saba rāma kathā nija nāma,

सुनत जुगल तन पुलक मन मगन सुमिरि गुन ग्राम ॥६॥

sunata jugala tana pulaka mana magana sumiri guna grāma. 6 .

प्रबिसि नगर कीजे सब काजा । हृदयँ राखि कोसलपुर राजा ॥
जपहिं नामु जन आरत भारी । मिटहिं कुसंकट होहिं सुखारी ॥
सियावर राम जय जय राम । मेरे प्रभु राम जय जय राम ॥

Thereupon Hanumān disclosed his identity and spoke to him of Shrī Rāma and his infinite virtues. As the name and glories of Rāma resounded in the air, a thrill of ecstasy ran through their bodies and their souls were drowned in an ocean of Bliss.

चौपाई-*caupāī:*

सुनहु पवनसुत रहनि हमारी । जिमि दसनन्हि महुँ जीभ बिचारी ॥
sunahu pavanasuta rahani hamārī, jimi dasananhi mahum̐ jībha bicārī .
तात कबहुँ मोहि जानि अनाथा । करिहहिं कृपा भानुकुल नाथा ॥
tāta kabahum̐ mohi jāni anāthā, karihahiṁ kṛpā bhānukula nāthā .
तामस तनु कछु साधन नाहीं । प्रीति न पद सरोज मन माहीं ॥
tāmasa tanu kachu sādhana nāhīṁ, prīti na pada saroja mana māhīṁ .
अब मोहि भा भरोस हनुमंता । बिनु हरिकृपा मिलहिं नहिं संता ॥
aba mohi bhā bharosa hanumaṁtā, binu harikṛpā milahiṁ nahiṁ saṁtā .
जौं रघुबीर अनुग्रह कीन्हा । तौ तुम्ह मोहि दरसु हठि दीन्हा ॥
jauṁ raghubīra anugraha kīnhā, tau tumha mohi darasu haṭhi dīnhā .
सुनहु बिभीषन प्रभु कै रीती । करहिं सदा सेवक पर प्रीती ॥
sunahu bibhīṣana prabhu kai rītī, karahiṁ sadā sevaka para prītī .
कहहु कवन मैं परम कुलीना । कपि चंचल सबहीं बिधि हीना ॥
kahahu kavana maiṁ parama kulīnā, kapi caṁcala sabahīṁ bidhi hīnā .
प्रात लेइ जो नाम हमारा । तेहि दिन ताहि न मिलै अहारा ॥
prāta lei jo nāma hamārā, tehi dina tāhi na milai ahārā .

As they conversed, Vibhishan said, “See O son-of-wind, how I dwell here! My plight is like that of the poor tongue that lies trapped behind the teeth. Tell me O friend, when will the Lord of Solar Dynasty shower his grace upon me—knowing me to be bereft and parentless? Alas, endowed as I am with this demoniac form, seeped in sin, I am unable to strive for Rāma or to cherish the love for his holy feet. But wait, now I do feel a hope in my heart—for today I have met you, and one can never meet a saint without the favor of the Lord. It is because Raghubīr was kind to me that this has come to pass: that you perforce revealed yourself to me.” Thereupon Hanumān said, “Listen Vibhishan, the Lord is ever affectionate to his devotees—for such is his very nature. Tell me, to what high birth can I lay any claim to—I am a frivolous monkey, vile in every way: a creature so unfortunate that even a mention of us in early mornings dooms its hearers to go without food the entire day.

जब तें रामु ब्याहि घर आए । नित नव मंगल मोद बधाए ॥
दीन दयाल बिरिदु संभारी । हरहु नाथ मम संकट भारी ॥
मंगल भवन अमंगल हारी । द्रवउ सो दसरथ अजिर बिहारी ॥

दोहा-*dohā:*

अस मैं अधम सखा सुनु मोहू पर रघुबीर ।
asa maiṁ adhama sakhā sunu mohū para raghubīra,
कीन्ही कृपा सुमिरि गुन भरे बिलोचन नीर ॥७॥
kīnhī kṛpā sumiri guna bhare bilocana nīra. 7 .

प्रबिसि नगर कीजे सब काजा । हृदयँ राखि कोसलपुर राजा ॥
जपहिं नामु जन आरत भारी । मिटहिं कुसंकट होहिं सुखारी ॥
सियावर राम जय जय राम । मेरे प्रभु राम जय जय राम ॥

And though I am so deplorable, yet O friend, Raghubīr has lavished his grace upon me." As he recalled the virtues of his Lord, Hanumān's eyes teared up.

Dt: ______________________

चौपाई-*caupāī:*

जानतहूँ अस स्वामि बिसारी । फिरहिं ते काहे न होहिं दुखारी ॥
jānatahūm̐ asa svāmi bisārī, phirahiṁ te kāhe na hohiṁ dukhārī .
एहि बिधि कहत राम गुन ग्रामा । पावा अनिर्बाच्य बिश्रामा ॥
ehi bidhi kahata rāma guna grāmā, pāvā anirbācya biśrāmā .
पुनि सब कथा बिभीषन कही । जेहि बिधि जनकसुता तहँ रही ॥
puni saba kathā bibhīṣana kahī, jehi bidhi janakasutā taham̐ rahī .
तब हनुमंत कहा सुनु भ्राता । देखी चहउँ जानकी माता ॥
taba hanumaṁta kahā sunu bhrātā, dekhī cahaum̐ jānakī mātā .
जुगुति बिभीषन सकल सुनाई । चलेउ पवनसुत बिदा कराई ॥
juguti bibhīṣana sakala sunāī, caleu pavanasuta bidā karāī .
करि सोइ रूप गयउ पुनि तहवाँ । बन असोक सीता रह जहवाँ ॥
kari soi rūpa gayau puni tahavām̐, bana asoka sītā raha jahavām̐ .
देखि मनहि महुँ कीन्ह प्रनामा । बैठेहिं बीति जात निसि जामा ॥
dekhi manahi mahum̐ kīnha pranāmā, baiṭhehiṁ bīti jāta nisi jāmā .
कृस तनु सीस जटा एक बेनी । जपति हृदयँ रघुपति गुन श्रेनी ॥
kṛsa tanu sīsa jaṭā eka benī, japati hṛdayam̐ raghupati guna śrenī .

Knowing of such a Lord and yet to forget him—to drift astray for this abject world—such unfortunate souls, no wonder, remain miserable [says Tulsī]. The two, recounting Rāma's infinite virtues, found an unspeakable calm descend upon their souls. Then Vibhishan narrated the whole episode and how Janak's daughter had been held captive there. And Hanumān said, "Listen brother, I wish to see Mother Sītā at once." Vibhishan detailed out the whole strategy, and the son-of-wind took his permission and left immediately. Assuming the same diminutive form as before, Hanumān repaired to the Ashoka-grove where Sītā was held confined. As soon as he saw Sītā from afar, he made obeisance to her mentally. It was evident that she had spent the long hours of the night sitting up. There she sat—emaciated in body, her hair knotted in a single braid upon her head—repeating to herself the list of Raghupati's perfections.

दोहा-*dohā:*

निज पद नयन दिएँ मन राम पद कमल लीन ।

nija pada nayana dieṁ mana rāma pada kamala līna,

परम दुखी भा पवनसुत देखि जानकी दीन ॥८॥

parama dukhī bhā pavanasuta dekhi jānakī dīna. 8 .

Sītā sat, her eyes fixed upon her feet—even as her mind was completely absorbed in the thought of Rāma's lotus feet. The son-of-wind became extremely distressed to see Janak's daughter so sad.

चौपाई-*caupāī:*

तरु पल्लव महुँ रहा लुकाई । करइ बिचार करौं का भाई ॥
taru pallava mahum̐ rahā lukāī, karai bicāra karaum̐ kā bhāī .
तेहि अवसर रावनु तहँ आवा । संग नारि बहु किएँ बनावा ॥
tehi avasara rāvanu taham̐ āvā, saṁga nāri bahu kiem̐ banāvā .
बहु बिधि खल सीतहि समुझावा । साम दान भय भेद देखावा ॥
bahu bidhi khala sītahi samujhāvā, sāma dāna bhaya bheda dekhāvā .
कह रावनु सुनु सुमुखि सयानी । मंदोदरी आदि सब रानी ॥
kaha rāvanu sunu sumukhi sayānī, maṁdodarī ādi saba rānī .
तव अनुचरीं करउँ पन मोरा । एक बार बिलोकु मम ओरा ॥
tava anucarīṁ karaum̐ pana morā, eka bāra biloku mama orā .
तृन धरि ओट कहति बैदेही । सुमिरि अवधपति परम सनेही ॥
tṛna dhari oṭa kahati baidehī, sumiri avadhapati parama sanehī .
सुनु दसमुख खद्योत प्रकासा । कबहुँ कि नलिनी करइ बिकासा ॥
sunu dasamukha khadyota prakāsā, kabahum̐ ki nalinī karai bikāsā .
अस मन समुझु कहति जानकी । खल सुधि नहिं रघुबीर बान की ॥
asa mana samujhu kahati jānakī, khala sudhi nahiṁ raghubīra bāna kī .
सठ सूनें हरि आनेहि मोही । अधम निलज्ज लाज नहिं तोही ॥
saṭha sūneṁ hari ānehi mohī, adhama nilajja lāja nahiṁ tohī .

Concealed behind the branches Hanumān thought to himself: “Come now brother, what ought I to do now?” At that very moment Rāvan arrived there—gaily adorned and with troops of women in tow. That wretch then tried to persuade Sītā, to maneuver her in every which way, by using tacts of blandishment, allurement, threat and misrepresentations: “Listen O fair lady, O beautiful faced,” he said, “I will make Mandodarī, and each of my queens, your handmaids—I swear to you—if only you will cast your glance my way just once.” Plucking a blade of grass in her hand and interposing it like her shield, and with her face averted, and with her thoughts fixed upon her own dear beloved Lord, Sītā said: “Hearken O ten-headed demon, when has a lotus ever bloomed in the light of glow-worm? You better deliberate carefully in your mind—for perhaps you have no idea what Raghubīr’s arrows are like—you wretch! You carried me off at a time when there was no one by my side. Don’t you feel ashamed of yourself, you vile impudent rogue!”

जब तें रामु ब्याहि घर आए । नित नव मंगल मोद बधाए ॥
दीन दयाल बिरिदु संभारी । हरहु नाथ मम संकट भारी ॥
मंगल भवन अमंगल हारी । द्रवउ सो दसरथ अजिर बिहारी ॥

दोहा-*dohā:*

आपुहि सुनि खद्योत सम रामहि भानु समान ।
āpuhi suni khadyota sama rāmahi bhānu samāna,
परुष बचन सुनि काढ़ि असि बोला अति खिसिआन ॥९॥
paruṣa bacana suni kāṛhi asi bolā ati khisiāna. 9 .

Hearing himself likened to a glow-worm and Shrī Rāma to the Sun, Rāvan felt much humiliated. Abashedly the monster drew his sword and spoke,

प्रबिसि नगर कीजे सब काजा । हृदयँ राखि कोसलपुर राजा ॥
जपहिं नामु जन आरत भारी । मिटहिं कुसंकट होहिं सुखारी ॥
सियावर राम जय जय राम । मेरे प्रभु राम जय जय राम ॥

चौपाई-*caupāī:*

सीता तैं मम कृत अपमाना । कटिहउँ तव सिर कठिन कृपाना ॥
sītā taiṁ mama kṛta apamānā, kaṭihaum̐ tava sira kaṭhina kṛpānā .
नाहिं त सपदि मानु मम बानी । सुमुखि होति न त जीवन हानी ॥
nāhiṁ ta sapadi mānu mama bānī, sumukhi hoti na ta jīvana hānī .
स्याम सरोज दाम सम सुंदर । प्रभु भुज करि कर सम दसकंधर ॥
syāma saroja dāma sama suṁdara,
prabhu bhuja kari kara sama dasakaṁdhara .
सो भुज कंठ कि तव असि घोरा । सुनु सठ अस प्रवान पन मोरा ॥
so bhuja kaṁṭha ki tava asi ghorā, sunu saṭha asa pravāna pana morā .
चंद्रहास हरु मम परितापं । रघुपति बिरह अनल संजातं ॥
caṁdrahāsa haru mama paritāpaṁ, raghupati biraha anala saṁjātaṁ .
सीतल निसित बहसि बर धारा । कह सीता हरु मम दुख भारा ॥
sītala nisita bahasi bara dhārā, kaha sītā haru mama dukha bhārā .
सुनत बचन पुनि मारन धावा । मयतनयाँ कहि नीति बुझावा ॥
sunata bacana puni mārana dhāvā, mayatanayām̐ kahi nīti bujhāvā .
कहेसि सकल निसिचरिन्ह बोलाई । सीतहि बहु बिधि त्रासहु जाई ॥
kahesi sakala nisicarinha bolāī, sītahi bahu bidhi trāsahu jāī .
मास दिवस महुँ कहा न माना । तौ मैं मारबि काढ़ि कृपाना ॥
māsa divasa mahum̐ kahā na mānā, tau maiṁ mārabi kāṛhi kṛpānā .

"Sītā, you insult me, be warned, I will forthwith cut your head with this very sword. Better obey my words—and you will be spared, beautiful faced—or prepare to lose your life at one." "Hearken you ten-headed monster! My own Lord's arms—that are beautiful as dark lotuses and mighty as an elephant's trunk—either they shall have my neck, or if not, then your cruel sword: that is my solemn vow, you wretch! O you gleaming scimitar, put an end to my suffering, and let this fiery anguish that I endure for Raghupati be quenched in the dark, cool, sharp edge of your blade; let me be rid of this burden of pain", cried Sītā. On hearing these words Rāvan again stepped forward to strike her but his queen Mandodarī, the daughter of Māyā, wisely restrained him with words of admonition. Rāvan then summoned all the female guards and ordained: "Torment her in every possible way; if she does not accept my proposal in a month's time, then with this very sword I shall behead her."

दोहा-dohā:

भवन गयउ दसकंधर इहाँ पिसाचिनि बृंद ।

bhavana gayau dasakaṁdhara ihāṁ pisācini bṛṁda,

सीतहि त्रास देखावहिं धरहिं रूप बहु मंद ॥१०॥

sītahi trāsa dekhāvahiṁ dharahiṁ rūpa bahu maṁda. 10.

Having instructed thusly, Rāvan returned to his palace; and the female Rākshas crew, assuming every kind of hideous form, proceeded to terrify and torture Sītā.

चौपाई-*caupāī:*

त्रिजटा नाम राच्छसी एका । राम चरन रति निपुन बिबेका ॥
trijaṭā nāma rācchasī ekā, rāma carana rati nipuna bibekā .
सबन्हौ बोलि सुनाएसि सपना । सीतहि सेइ करहु हित अपना ॥
sabanhau boli sunāesi sapanā, sītahi sei karahu hita apanā .
सपनें बानर लंका जारी । जातुधान सेना सब मारी ॥
sapaneṁ bānara laṁkā jārī, jātudhāna senā saba mārī .
खर आरूढ़ नगन दससीसा । मुंडित सिर खंडित भुज बीसा ॥
k͟hara ārūṛha nagana dasasīsā, muṁḍita sira khaṁḍita bhuja bīsā .
एहि बिधि सो दच्छिन दिसि जाई । लंका मनहुँ बिभीषन पाई ॥
ehi bidhi so dacchina disi jāī, laṁkā manahum̐ bibhīṣana pāī .
नगर फिरी रघुबीर दोहाई । तब प्रभु सीता बोलि पठाई ॥
nagara phirī raghubīra dohāī, taba prabhu sītā boli paṭhāī .
यह सपना मैं कहउँ पुकारी । होइहि सत्य गएँ दिन चारी ॥
yaha sapanā maiṁ kahaum̐ pukārī, hoihi satya gaem̐ dina cārī .
तासु बचन सुनि ते सब डरीं । जनकसुता के चरनन्हि परीं ॥
tāsu bacana suni te saba ḍarīṁ, janakasutā ke carananhi parīṁ .

But there was one amongst them, Trijatā by name, who was devoted to the lotus feet of Rāma and very prudent and wise. Gathering them all around her she told them of her dream and she exhorted them to serve Sītā if they truly cared for their welfare saying, "I had this dream, and in my dream I saw a monkey set fire to Lankā and kill the whole army of Rākshas; and I also saw the Ten-headed Rāvan, mounted on a donkey, all naked, with his heads shorn, and his twenty arms chopped; and in that manner I saw him ride towards the south; and then it appears as if Vibhishan inherits Lankā; and with the resounding of drums, the victory of Shrī Rāma is proclaimed throughout the land and Sītā is reunited with her Lord. This dream, I tell you, will come true within a few days time." Hearing such prophetic words, all became terrified and threw themselves at Sītā's feet.

दोहा-dohā:

जहँ तहँ गईं सकल तब सीता कर मन सोच ।
jahaṁ tahaṁ gaīṁ sakala taba sītā kara mana soca,
मास दिवस बीतें मोहि मारिहि निसिचर पोच ॥११॥
māsa divasa bīteṁ mohi mārihi nisicara poca. 11 .

Then they all scurried away, each going her own way; and Sītā thought to herself, "This vile monster will slay me at the end of a long month."

Dt: ______________

चौपाई-*caupāī:*

त्रिजटा सन बोलीं कर जोरी । मातु बिपति संगिनि तैं मोरी ॥
trijaṭā sana bolīṁ kara jorī, mātu bipati saṁgini taiṁ morī .

तजौं देह करु बेगि उपाई । दुसहु बिरहु अब नहिं सहि जाई ॥
tajauṁ deha karu begi upāī, dusahu birahu aba nahiṁ sahi jāī .

आनि काठ रचु चिता बनाई । मातु अनल पुनि देहि लगाई ॥
āni kāṭha racu citā banāī, mātu anala puni dehi lagāī .

सत्य करहि मम प्रीति सयानी । सुनै को श्रवन सूल सम बानी ॥
satya karahi mama prīti sayānī, sunai ko śravana sūla sama bānī .

सुनत बचन पद गहि समुझाएसि । प्रभु प्रताप बल सुजसु सुनाएसि ॥
sunata bacana pada gahi samujhāesi, prabhu pratāpa bala sujasu sunāesi .

निसि न अनल मिल सुनु सुकुमारी । अस कहि सो निज भवन सिधारी ॥
nisi na anala mila sunu sukumārī, asa kahi so nija bhavana sidhārī .

कह सीता बिधि भा प्रतिकूला । मिलिहि न पावक मिटिहि न सूला ॥
kaha sītā bidhi bhā pratikūlā, milihi na pāvaka miṭihi na sūlā .

देखिअत प्रगट गगन अंगारा । अवनि न आवत एकउ तारा ॥
dekhiata pragaṭa gagana aṁgārā, avani na āvata ekau tārā .

पावकमय ससि स्रवत न आगी । मानहुँ मोहि जानि हत भागी ॥
pāvakamaya sasi sravata na āgī, mānahuṁ mohi jāni hata bhāgī .

सुनहि बिनय मम बिटप असोका । सत्य नाम करु हरु मम सोका ॥
sunahi binaya mama biṭapa asokā, satya nāma karu haru mama sokā .

नूतन किसलय अनल समाना । देहि अगिनि जनि करहि निदाना ॥
nūtana kisalaya anala samānā, dehi agini jani karahi nidānā .

देखि परम बिरहाकुल सीता । सो छन कपिहि कलप सम बीता ॥
dekhi parama birahākula sītā, so chana kapihi kalapa sama bītā .

Then with joined palms she spoke to Trijatā, "O mother, in my plight you are the only help at this hour. Quick, devise some plan whereby I may be rid of this life. This bereavement of mine is intolerable and can no longer be endured. This wood I gather into a funeral pyre—get some fire to light it and make verity of my true love for my Lord, O wise one. The words of Rāvan pierce my ears like a lance—who can listen to that?" Upon hearing this Trijatā clasped Sītā by the feet and dissuaded her from doing so. She comforted her and recounted to her the might, majesty, and glory of Shrī Rāma. Finally saying, "Listen O Tender-one, no fire can be had at night", she too left for her home.

जब तें रामु ब्याहि घर आए । नित नव मंगल मोद बधाए ॥
दीन दयाल बिरिदु संभारी । हरहु नाथ मम संकट भारी ॥
मंगल भवन अमंगल हारी । द्रवउ सो दसरथ अजिर बिहारी ॥

सोरठा-*soraṭhā:*

कपि करि हृदयँ बिचार दीन्हि मुद्रिका डारि तब ।
kapi kari hṛdayam̐ bicāra dīnhi mudrikā ḍāri taba,
जनु असोक अंगार दीन्ह हरषि उठि कर गहेउ ॥१२॥
janu asoka aṁgāra dīnha haraṣi uṭhi kara gaheu. 12 .

प्रबिसि नगर कीजे सब काजा । हृदयँ राखि कोसलपुर राजा ॥
जपहिं नामु जन आरत भारी । मिटहिं कुसंकट होहिं सुखारी ॥
सियावर राम जय जय राम । मेरे प्रभु राम जय जय राम ॥

And Sītā said to herself, “Heaven itself is so unkind. There is no fire to be had and I cannot be cured of my agony otherwise. Alas, sparks of fire are visible everywhere in the sky, but not a single star drops down below to burn my pyre! The moon is all ablaze but refuses to rain down sparks, as if knowing what a poor wretch I am. Hear my prayer, ye Ashoka trees, answer to your name and rid me of this pain: let your flame colored buds supply me with the fire to consume this body so that this agony of mine shall end.” When Hanumān saw Sītā in bereavement, lamenting so piteously, every moment to him passed like an age.
After considerable thought, Hanumān then let the signet ring of Shri Rāma drop down below—as though a spark had fallen from the Ashoka. Sītā started up with joy and clasped the ring in her hands.

Dt: ______________________________

चौपाई-*caupāī:*

तब देखी मुद्रिका मनोहर । राम नाम अंकित अति सुंदर ॥
taba dekhī mudrikā manohara, rāma nāma aṁkita ati suṁdara .
चकित चितव मुदरी पहिचानी । हरष बिषाद हृदयँ अकुलानी ॥
cakita citava mudarī pahicānī, haraṣa biṣāda hṛdayaṁ akulānī .
जीति को सकइ अजय रघुराई । माया तें असि रचि नहिं जाई ॥
jīti ko sakai ajaya raghurāī, māyā teṁ asi raci nahiṁ jāī .
सीता मन बिचार कर नाना । मधुर बचन बोलेउ हनुमाना ॥
sītā mana bicāra kara nānā, madhura bacana boleu hanumānā .
रामचंद्र गुन बरनैं लागा । सुनतहिं सीता कर दुख भागा ॥
rāmacaṁdra guna baranaiṁ lāgā, sunatahiṁ sītā kara dukha bhāgā .
लागीं सुनैं श्रवन मन लाई । आदिहु तें सब कथा सुनाई ॥
lāgīṁ sunaiṁ śravana mana lāī, ādihu teṁ saba kathā sunāī .
श्रवनामृत जेहिं कथा सुहाई । कही सो प्रगट होति किन भाई ॥
śravanāmṛta jehiṁ kathā suhāī, kahī so pragaṭa hoti kina bhāī .
तब हनुमंत निकट चलि गयऊ । फिरि बैठीं मन बिसमय भयऊ ॥
taba hanumaṁta nikaṭa cali gayaū, phiri baiṭhīṁ mana bisamaya bhayaū .
राम दूत मैं मातु जानकी । सत्य सपथ करुनानिधान की ॥
rāma dūta maiṁ mātu jānakī, satya sapatha karunānidhāna kī .
यह मुद्रिका मातु मैं आनी । दीन्हि राम तुम्ह कहँ सहिदानी ॥
yaha mudrikā mātu maiṁ ānī, dīnhi rāma tumha kahaṁ sahidānī .
नर बानरहि संग कहु कैसें । कही कथा भइ संगति जैसें ॥
nara bānarahi saṁga kahu kaiseṁ, kahī kathā bhai saṁgati jaiseṁ .

As she examined the lovely ring engraved with the beautiful name Rāma, Sītā recognized it immediately to be her Lord's; and she was full of amazement; and her heart fluttered with a mingled joy and sorrow. "Who can conquer the unconquerable Raghurai [part the ring away from him]? And yet such a ring cannot be fabricated by Māyā's trickery"—Sītā was thinking in that vein and all sorts of fancies passed through her straitened mind when Hanumān, in a most honeyed accent, began to recount Shri Rāmachandra's praises. As Sītā listened her grief took to flight; and intently she hearkened, with her ears and her soul, to the voice which narrated the story of Rāma from the very start. "O brother, whosoever related this chronicle—which is like nectar to my ears—why not reveal yourself?" said Sītā when it was over.

जब तें रामु ब्याहि घर आए । नित नव मंगल मोद बधाए ॥
दीन दयाल बिरिदु संभारी । हरहु नाथ मम संकट भारी ॥
मंगल भवन अमंगल हारी । द्रवउ सो दसरथ अजिर बिहारी ॥

दोहा-*dohā:*

कपि के बचन सप्रेम सुनि उपजा मन बिस्वास ।
kapi ke bacana saprema suni upajā mana bisvāsa,
जाना मन क्रम बचन यह कृपासिंधु कर दास ॥ १३ ॥
jānā mana krama bacana yaha kṛpāsiṁdhu kara dāsa. 13 .

प्रबिसि नगर कीजे सब काजा । हृदयँ राखि कोसलपुर राजा ॥
जपहिं नामु जन आरत भारी । मिटहिं कुसंकट होहिं सुखारी ॥
सियावर राम जय जय राम । मेरे प्रभु राम जय जय राम ॥

Thereupon Hanumān revealed himself and drew near. Seeing that it was a monkey Sītā averted her face and sat down in complete amazement. "O mother Jānakī, I am the messenger of Shrī Rāma—truly I swear to you by the All-merciful Lord Himself. It was I who brought this ring; Shrī Rāma gave it to me as a token for you." "But what would bring such fellowship between men and monkey, first say", said Sītā. Then Hanumān explained the circumstance which had wrought that strange conjugation.
As Sītā heard the affectionate speech of the monkey, her soul began to trust in him. She recognized Hanumān to be the faithful servant of the All-merciful in thought, word, and deed.

चौपाई-*caupāī:*

हरिजन जानि प्रीति अति गाढ़ी । सजल नयन पुलकावलि बाढ़ी ॥
harijana jāni prīti ati gāṛhī, sajala nayana pulakāvali bāṛhī .
बूडत बिरह जलधि हनुमाना । भयहु तात मो कहुँ जलजाना ॥
būṛata biraha jaladhi hanumānā, bhayahu tāta mo kahum̐ jalajānā .
अब कहु कुसल जाउँ बलिहारी । अनुज सहित सुख भवन खरारी ॥
aba kahu kusala jāum̐ balihārī, anuja sahita sukha bhavana kharārī .
कोमलचित कृपाल रघुराई । कपि केहि हेतु धरी निठुराई ॥
komalacita kṛpāla raghurāī, kapi kehi hetu dharī niṭhurāī .
सहज बानि सेवक सुख दायक । कबहुँक सुरति करत रघुनायक ॥
sahaja bāni sevaka sukha dāyaka, kabahum̐ka surati karata raghunāyaka .
कबहुँ नयन मम सीतल ताता । होइहहिं निरखि स्याम मृदु गाता ॥
kabahum̐ nayana mama sītala tātā, hoihahiṁ nirakhi syāma mṛdu gātā .
बचनु न आव नयन भरे बारी । अहह नाथ हौं निपट बिसारी ॥
bacanu na āva nayana bhare bārī, ahaha nātha hauṁ nipaṭa bisārī .
देखि परम बिरहाकुल सीता । बोला कपि मृदु बचन बिनीता ॥
dekhi parama birahākula sītā, bolā kapi mṛdu bacana binītā .
मातु कुसल प्रभु अनुज समेता । तव दुख दुखी सुकृपा निकेता ॥
mātu kusala prabhu anuja sametā, tava dukha dukhī sukṛpā niketā .
जनि जननी मानहु जियँ ऊना । तुम्ह ते प्रेमु राम कें दूना ॥
jani jananī mānahu jiyam̐ ūnā, tumha te premu rāma keṁ dūnā .

Knowing him to be a devotee of the Lord Sītā developed an intense affection for him, and her eyes filled over with tears, and a thrill ran through her body as she spoke, "I was sinking in the ocean of bereavement, O Hanumān, but now in you I have found a bark. I beseech of thee to please tell me of their welfare, son. Please tell me that the blessed Kharari, along with his brother, is alright and well. Wherefore has the tender-hearted compassionate Lord of Raghus become so hard-hearted? Whose very nature it is to impart bliss to his devotees—am I even remembered by our Lord? Will my eyes, O son, be gladdened again by the sight of his exquisite swarthy form?" Words failed her and her eyes swam in tears, "Alas! My Lord has entirely forgotten me."

जब तें रामु ब्याहि घर आए । नित नव मंगल मोद बधाए ॥
दीन दयाल बिरिदु संभारी । हरहु नाथ मम संकट भारी ॥
मंगल भवन अमंगल हारी । द्रवउ सो दसरथ अजिर बिहारी ॥

दोहा-dohā:

रघुपति कर संदेसु अब सुनु जननी धरि धीर ।
raghupati kara saṁdesu aba sunu jananī dhari dhīra,
अस कहि कपि गदगद भयउ भरे बिलोचन नीर ॥ १४ ॥
asa kahi kapi gadagada bhayau bhare bilocana nīra. 14 .

प्रबिसि नगर कीजे सब काजा । हृदयँ राखि कोसलपुर राजा ॥
जपहिं नामु जन आरत भारी । मिटहिं कुसंकट होहिं सुखारी ॥
सियावर राम जय जय राम । मेरे प्रभु राम जय जय राम ॥

Seeing Sītā sorely distressed—in intense bereavement of separation from her Lord—the monkey spoke in soothing gentle tones, “The Lord and his brother are both well, my mother—except that the All-merciful is very sorrowful in your sorrow. Do not feel disquieted O mother; do be assured that Rāma’s love for you is twice as great as yours.
Now compose yourself and take heart, mother, and hearken to the message of Raghupati.” Even as he spoke, the monkey’s voice choked with emotions and his eyes were filled with tears.

चौपाई-*caupāī:*

कहेउ राम बियोग तव सीता । मो कहुँ सकल भए बिपरीता ॥
kaheu rāma biyoga tava sītā, mo kahum̐ sakala bhae biparītā .
नव तरु किसलय मनहुँ कृसानू । काल निसा सम निसि ससि भानू ॥
nava taru kisalaya manahum̐ kṛsānū, kāla nisā sama nisi sasi bhānū .
कुबलय बिपिन कुंत बन सरिसा । बारिद तपत तेल जनु बरिसा ॥
kubalaya bipina kuṁta bana sarisā, bārida tapata tela janu barisā .
जे हित रहे करत तेइ पीरा । उरग स्वास सम त्रिबिध समीरा ॥
je hita rahe karata tei pīrā, uraga svāsa sama tribidha samīrā .
कहेहू तें कछु दुख घटि होई । काहि कहौं यह जान न कोई ॥
kahehū teṁ kachu dukha ghaṭi hoī, kāhi kahauṁ yaha jāna na koī .
तत्व प्रेम कर मम अरु तोरा । जानत प्रिया एकु मनु मोरा ॥
tatva prema kara mama aru torā, jānata priyā eku manu morā .
सो मनु सदा रहत तोहि पाहीं । जानु प्रीति रसु एतनेहि माहीं ॥
so manu sadā rahata tohi pāhīṁ, jānu prīti rasu etanehi māhīṁ .
प्रभु संदेसु सुनत बैदेही । मगन प्रेम तन सुधि नहिं तेही ॥
prabhu saṁdesu sunata baidehī, magana prema tana sudhi nahiṁ tehī .
कह कपि हृदयँ धीर धरु माता । सुमिरु राम सेवक सुखदाता ॥
kaha kapi hṛdayam̐ dhīra dharu mātā, sumiru rāma sevaka sukhadātā .
उर आनहु रघुपति प्रभुताई । सुनि मम बचन तजहु कदराई ॥
ura ānahu raghupati prabhutāī, suni mama bacana tajahu kadarāī .

"Here is what Shrī Rāma has conveyed: 'Ever since I have been separated from you, O Sītā, everything to me has become its very reverse. The budding tender foliage on trees looks to me like tongues of fire; the night appears dreadful as the night of final dissolution; the moon scorches like the sun; fields of lotuses appear like so many spears impaled on the ground; the rain-clouds appear to pour down roiling oil. That which comforted before, now torments; and the cool, soft, fragrant breezes are now like the fiery breaths of serpents. Sharing is said to relieve anguish but to whom can I say?—for there is no one who will understand. The essence of love which binds you to me is known only to my own soul, O dear. My heart ever abides with you…—from afar know of my love for you with just these words.'" As Vaidehī listened to Rāma's message she was overwhelmed with love and lost all sense of body consciousness. The monkey spoke again, "O mother, please collect yourself, take heart, and fix your mind upon Shrī Rāma—remembering him as the benefactor of his devotees. Reflect upon his might, listen to my words, and cast away all anxiety.

जब तें रामु ब्याहि घर आए । नित नव मंगल मोद बधाए ॥
दीन दयाल बिरिदु संभारी । हरहु नाथ मम संकट भारी ॥
मंगल भवन अमंगल हारी । द्रवउ सो दसरथ अजिर बिहारी ॥

दोहा-dohā:

निसिचर निकर पतंग सम रघुपति बान कृसानु ।
nisicara nikara pataṁga sama raghupati bāna kṛsānu,
जननी हृदयँ धीर धरु जरे निसाचर जानु ॥१५॥
jananī hṛdayaṁ dhīra dharu jare nisācara jānu. 15 .

प्रबिसि नगर कीजे सब काजा । हृदयँ राखि कोसलपुर राजा ॥
जपहिं नामु जन आरत भारी । मिटहिं कुसंकट होहिं सुखारी ॥
सियावर राम जय जय राम । मेरे प्रभु राम जय जय राम ॥

To the flames of Raghupati's shafts, the demons are just like so many moths; take them to be incinerated already; have courage, O mother.

Dt: ____________________

चौपाई-*caupāī:*

जौं रघुबीर होति सुधि पाई । करते नहिं बिलंबु रघुराई ॥
jauṁ raghubīra hoti sudhi pāī, karate nahiṁ bilaṁbu raghurāī .
राम बान रबि उएँ जानकी । तम बरूथ कहँ जातुधान की ॥
rāma bāna rabi ueṁ jānakī, tama barūtha kahaṁ jātudhāna kī .
अबहिं मातु मैं जाउँ लवाई । प्रभु आयसु नहिं राम दोहाई ॥
abahiṁ mātu maiṁ jāuṁ lavāī, prabhu āyasu nahiṁ rāma dohāī .
कछुक दिवस जननी धरु धीरा । कपिन्ह सहित अइहहिं रघुबीरा ॥
kachuka divasa jananī dharu dhīrā, kapinha sahita aihahiṁ raghubīrā .
निसिचर मारि तोहि लै जैहहिं । तिहुँ पुर नारदादि जसु गैहहिं ॥
nisicara māri tohi lai jaihahiṁ, tihuṁ pura nāradādi jasu gaihahiṁ .
हैं सुत कपि सब तुम्हहि समाना । जातुधान अति भट बलवाना ॥
haiṁ suta kapi saba tumhahi samānā, jātudhāna ati bhaṭa balavānā .
मोरें हृदय परम संदेहा । सुनि कपि प्रगट कीन्हि निज देहा ॥
moreṁ hṛdaya parama saṁdehā, suni kapi pragaṭa kīnhi nija dehā .
कनक भूधराकार सरीरा । समर भयंकर अतिबल बीरा ॥
kanaka bhūdharākāra sarīrā, samara bhayaṁkara atibala bīrā .
सीता मन भरोस तब भयऊ । पुनि लघु रूप पवनसुत लयऊ ॥
sītā mana bharosa taba bhayaū, puni laghu rūpa pavanasuta layaū .

If Raghubīr had known your whereabouts he wouldn't have delayed. Now know this: To disperse the darkness of demon hosts, the fiery shafts of Rāma—alike the brilliant rays of rising Sun—are about to appear on the horizon. I myself could take you now mother but—I swear to you by Rāma—I haven't received any orders for that. Be patient for just a few days more and Shrī Rāma will himself arrive along with the army of monkeys. Killing the demons he will rescue you; and Nārad and others will get to sing the Lord's glories in the three spheres of creation for all times to come." "Are all the monkeys just like you, my son? The demon warriors are huge and powerful, and my heart becomes rather doubtful [when I envision the contrast]." Upon hearing that Hanumān revealed himself in his natural form: colossal as a mountain of gold, terrible in battle, possessing vast might, gallant, replete with valor. Sītā took comfort at the sight and the son-of-wind once again resumed his diminutive form.

जब तें रामु ब्याहि घर आए । नित नव मंगल मोद बधाए ॥
दीन दयाल बिरिदु संभारी । हरहु नाथ मम संकट भारी ॥
मंगल भवन अमंगल हारी । द्रवउ सो दसरथ अजिर बिहारी ॥

दोहा-*dohā:*

सुनु माता साखामृग नहिं बल बुद्धि बिसाल ।
sunu mātā sākhāmṛga nahiṁ bala buddhi bisāla,
प्रभु प्रताप तें गरुड़हि खाइ परम लघु ब्याल ॥१६॥
prabhu pratāpa teṁ garuṛahi khāi parama laghu byāla. 16 .

प्रबिसि नगर कीजे सब काजा । हृदयँ राखि कोसलपुर राजा ॥
जपहिं नामु जन आरत भारी । मिटहिं कुसंकट होहिं सुखारी ॥
सियावर राम जय जय राम । मेरे प्रभु राम जय जय राम ॥

"Hearken mother, we monkeys have no great strength or wit of our own, but by the favor of Lord Rāma even a snake—small as it is—might swallow a Garuda."

Dt: ______________________

चौपाई-*caupāī:*

मन संतोष सुनत कपि बानी । भगति प्रताप तेज बल सानी ॥
mana saṁtoṣa sunata kapi bānī, bhagati pratāpa teja bala sānī .
आसिष दीन्हि रामप्रिय जाना । होहु तात बल सील निधाना ॥
āsiṣa dīnhi rāmapriya jānā, hohu tāta bala sīla nidhānā .
अजर अमर गुननिधि सुत होहू । करहुँ बहुत रघुनायक छोहू ॥
ajara amara gunanidhi suta hohū, karahum̐ bahuta raghunāyaka chohū .
करहुँ कृपा प्रभु अस सुनि काना । निर्भर प्रेम मगन हनुमाना ॥
karahum̐ kṛpā prabhu asa suni kānā, nirbhara prema magana hanumānā .
बार बार नाएसि पद सीसा । बोला बचन जोरि कर कीसा ॥
bāra bāra nāesi pada sīsā, bolā bacana jori kara kīsā .
अब कृतकृत्य भयउँ मैं माता । आसिष तव अमोघ बिख्याता ॥
aba kṛtakṛtya bhayaum̐ maiṁ mātā, āsiṣa tava amogha bikhyātā .
सुनहु मातु मोहि अतिसय भूखा । लागि देखि सुंदर फल रूखा ॥
sunahu mātu mohi atisaya bhūkhā, lāgi dekhi suṁdara phala rūkhā .
सुनु सुत करहिं बिपिन रखवारी । परम सुभट रजनीचर भारी ॥
sunu suta karahiṁ bipina rakhavārī, parama subhaṭa rajanīcara bhārī .
तिन्ह कर भय माता मोहि नाहीं । जौं तुम्ह सुख मानहु मन माहीं ॥
tinha kara bhaya mātā mohi nāhīṁ, jauṁ tumha sukha mānahu mana māhīṁ .

Sītā felt gratified in her heart as she hearkened to the monkey's words—full of devotion and so revealing of the might and majesty of her Lord. Recognizing Hanumān to be the beloved of Shrī Rāma, Sītā showered upon him her choicest blessings: "May you become the very monument of virtue and might, my son! May you become ageless, deathless and a treasure-house of every good quality. And my son, may the Lord of Raghus ever remain abundantly gracious to you." 'That the Lord will ever shower his grace'—hearing this Hanumān became utterly overwhelmed with emotion. Again and again he bowed his head at mother Sītā's feet and with folded hands said, "Now I have found everything I ever need in life, my mother, for your blessing is completely unfailing—this the whole world knows." Then recovering, the monkey said, "Listen mother I am frightfully hungry, especially seeing these trees laden with delicious fruits." "Listen son, this grove is guarded by the most formidable terrible monsters." "Mother, I have no fear of them; if you feel easy in your heart and approve, then just say the word."

दोहा-dohā:

देखि बुद्धि बल निपुन कपि कहेउ जानकीं जाहु ।
dekhi buddhi bala nipuna kapi kaheu jānakīṁ jāhu,
रघुपति चरन हृदयँ धरि तात मधुर फल खाहु ॥१७॥
raghupati carana hṛdayam̐ dhari tāta madhura phala khāhu. 17 .

Seeing that the monkey was perfect in strength and sagacity, Jānakī said: "Fixing your heart upon Lord Raghupati's holy feet, go partake of these delicious fruits, son."

चौपाई-*caupāī:*

चलेउ नाइ सिरु पैठेउ बागा । फल खाएसि तरु तोरैं लागा ॥
caleu nāi siru paiṭheu bāgā, phala khāesi taru toraiṁ lāgā .
रहे तहाँ बहु भट रखवारे । कछु मारेसि कछु जाइ पुकारे ॥
rahe tahām̐ bahu bhaṭa rakhavāre, kachu māresi kachu jāi pukāre .
नाथ एक आवा कपि भारी । तेहिं असोक बाटिका उजारी ॥
nātha eka āvā kapi bhārī, tehiṁ asoka bāṭikā ujārī .
खाएसि फल अरु बिटप उपारे । रच्छक मर्दि मर्दि महि डारे ॥
khāesi phala aru biṭapa upāre, racchaka mardi mardi mahi ḍāre .
सुनि रावन पठए भट नाना । तिन्हहि देखि गर्जेउ हनुमाना ॥
suni rāvana paṭhae bhaṭa nānā, tinhahi dekhi garjeu hanumānā .
सब रजनीचर कपि संघारे । गए पुकारत कछु अधमारे ॥
saba rajanīcara kapi saṁghāre, gae pukārata kachu adhamāre .
पुनि पठयउ तेहिं अच्छकुमारा । चला संग लै सुभट अपारा ॥
puni paṭhayau tehiṁ acchakumārā, calā saṁga lai subhaṭa apārā .
आवत देखि बिटप गहि तर्जा । ताहि निपाति महाधुनि गर्जा ॥
āvata dekhi biṭapa gahi tarjā, tāhi nipāti mahādhuni garjā .

Bowing his head Hanumān left and entered the grove; there he ate the fruits and many a tree he broke. Of the several warriors posted there as guards, some were killed by Hanumān while the rest took to flight and yelped for help, "O lord, an enormous monkey has come and laid waste to the whole Ashoka-grove. He has eaten fruits, uprooted trees, and mauled many guards, mashing them into the ground." Hearing that, Rāvan immediately dispatched several fighters. At the sight of them Hanumān roared like thunder and slaughtered them all. A few that survived—more dead than alive—bolted away screaming. Rāvan then sent his young prince Akshya, who took with him a vast number of his very best warriors. Seeing them approach Hanumān seized a tree, brandishing which he killed the prince in one fell swoop—and then Hanumān let out a terrible roar.

दोहा-dohā:

कछु मारेसि कछु मर्देसि कछु मिलएसि धरि धूरि ।
kachu māresi kachu mardesi kachu milaesi dhari dhūri,
कछु पुनि जाइ पुकारे प्रभु मर्कट बल भूरि ॥१८॥
kachu puni jāi pukāre prabhu markaṭa bala bhūri. 18 .

And of the remaining army, some Hanumān mangled, some he crushed, some he laid low in the dust; some again fled to Rāvan and cried, "O lord, the monkey is much too strong for us."

जब तें रामु ब्याहि घर आए । नित नव मंगल मोद बधाए ॥
दीन दयाल बिरिदु संभारी । हरहु नाथ मम संकट भारी ॥
मंगल भवन अमंगल हारी । द्रवउ सो दसरथ अजिर बिहारी ॥

प्रबिसि नगर कीजे सब काजा । हृदयँ राखि कोसलपुर राजा ॥
जपहिं नामु जन आरत भारी । मिटहिं कुसंकट होहिं सुखारी ॥
सियावर राम जय जय राम । मेरे प्रभु राम जय जय राम ॥

चौपाई-caupāī:

सुनि सुत बध लंकेस रिसाना । पठएसि मेघनाद बलवाना ॥
suni suta badha laṁkesa risānā, paṭhaesi meghanāda balavānā .
मारसि जनि सुत बांधेसु ताही । देखिअ कपिहि कहाँ कर आही ॥
mārasi jani suta bāṁdhesu tāhī, dekhia kapihi kahām̐ kara āhī .
चला इंद्रजित अतुलित जोधा । बंधु निधन सुनि उपजा क्रोधा ॥
calā iṁdrajita atulita jodhā, baṁdhu nidhana suni upajā krodhā .
कपि देखा दारुन भट आवा । कटकटाइ गर्जा अरु धावा ॥
kapi dekhā dāruna bhaṭa āvā, kaṭakaṭāi garjā aru dhāvā .
अति बिसाल तरु एक उपारा । बिरथ कीन्ह लंकेस कुमारा ॥
ati bisāla taru eka upārā, biratha kīnha laṁkesa kumārā .
रहे महाभट ताके संगा । गहि गहि कपि मर्दइ निज अंगा ॥
rahe mahābhaṭa tāke saṁgā, gahi gahi kapi mardai nija aṁgā .
तिन्हहि निपाति ताहि सन बाजा । भिरे जुगल मानहुँ गजराजा ॥
tinhahi nipāti tāhi sana bājā, bhire jugala mānahum̐ gajarājā .
मुठिका मारि चढ़ा तरु जाई । ताहि एक छन मुरुछा आई ॥
muṭhikā māri caṛhā taru jāī, tāhi eka chana muruchā āī .
उठि बहोरि कीन्हिसि बहु माया । जीति न जाइ प्रभंजन जाया ॥
uṭhi bahori kīnhisi bahu māyā, jīti na jāi prabhaṁjana jāyā .

The King of Lankā flew into rage when he learnt of his son's death and sent his most valiant son Meghnād. "Do not kill him son, but bind him and bring him here; I would fain see this monkey and where he comes from." With many excellent warriors, the conqueror of Indra tore forward—a peerless champion, full of burning fury at the tidings of his brother's death. When Hanumān saw a formidable chieftain approaching this time, he gnashed his teeth and hollering frightfully lunged at him. Uprooting an enormous tree he smashed it down on the chariot—rendering the crown prince of Lankā chariot-less. The mighty warriors who had accompanied the prince were seized one by one by Hanumān and crushed under his limbs. Having finished them off, he again closeted with Meghnād—and verily it was an encounter of two lordly elephants. After dealing him a deadly blow, Hanumān sprang and climbed upon a tree. Meghnād lay unconscious for a few moments and then rose up to fight again—this time resorting to delusive tricks of wizardry—but the son-of-wind was not to be vanquished.

दोहा-dohā:

ब्रह्म अस्त्र तेहिं साँधा कपि मन कीन्ह बिचार ।

brahma astra tehiṁ sām̐dhā kapi mana kīnha bicāra,

जौं न ब्रह्मसर मानउँ महिमा मिटइ अपार ॥ १९ ॥

jauṁ na brahmasara mānaum̐ mahimā miṭai apāra. 19 .

Finally Meghnād made ready with the invincible Brahmāstra. At that the monkey thought to himself: "If I do not submit to Brahmmā's shaft, its infinite fame will have come to naught."

जब तें रामु ब्याहि घर आए । नित नव मंगल मोद बधाए ॥
दीन दयाल बिरिदु संभारी । हरहु नाथ मम संकट भारी ॥
मंगल भवन अमंगल हारी । द्रवउ सो दसरथ अजिर बिहारी ॥

प्रबिसि नगर कीजे सब काजा । हृदयँ राखि कोसलपुर राजा ॥
जपहिं नामु जन आरत भारी । मिटहिं कुसंकट होहिं सुखारी ॥
सियावर राम जय जय राम । मेरे प्रभु राम जय जय राम ॥

चौपाई-*caupāī:*

ब्रह्मबान कपि कहुँ तेहिं मारा । परतिहुँ बार कटकु संघारा ॥
brahmabāna kapi kahuṁ tehiṁ mārā, paratihuṁ bāra kaṭaku saṁghārā .
तेहिं देखा कपि मुरुछित भयऊ । नागपास बाँधेसि लै गयऊ ॥
tehiṁ dekhā kapi muruchita bhayaū, nāgapāsa bāṁdhesi lai gayaū .
जासु नाम जपि सुनहु भवानी । भव बंधन काटहिं नर ग्यानी ॥
jāsu nāma japi sunahu bhavānī, bhava baṁdhana kāṭahiṁ nara gyānī .
तासु दूत कि बंध तरु आवा । प्रभु कारज लगि कपिहिं बँधावा ॥
tāsu dūta ki baṁdha taru āvā, prabhu kāraja lagi kapihiṁ baṁdhāvā .
कपि बंधन सुनि निसिचर धाए । कौतुक लागि सभाँ सब आए ॥
kapi baṁdhana suni nisicara dhāe, kautuka lāgi sabhāṁ saba āe .
दसमुख सभा दीखि कपि जाई । कहि न जाइ कछु अति प्रभुताई ॥
dasamukha sabhā dīkhi kapi jāī, kahi na jāi kachu ati prabhutāī .
कर जोरें सुर दिसिप बिनीता । भृकुटि बिलोकत सकल सभीता ॥
kara joreṁ sura disipa binītā, bhṛkuṭi bilokata sakala sabhītā .
देखि प्रताप न कपि मन संका । जिमि अहिगन महुँ गरुड़ असंका ॥
dekhi pratāpa na kapi mana saṁkā, jimi ahigana mahuṁ garuṛa asaṁkā .

Meghnād launched the Brahmāstra against Hanumān and he fell—taking down the whole demon host as he went crashing. Seeing that the monkey was in a swoon, Meghnād tied him up in the Serpent-Noose and carried him away. Observe, O Bhavānī [said Shiva], how the emissary of Rāma—by the repetition of whose very name the fetters of worldly bondages are rent asunder—today himself became ensnared it would seem. But in reality it was in the service to his Lord that Hanumān submitted himself to be thusly bound. The citizens, upon hearing that the monkey had finally been caught, all rushed to enjoy the spectacle. There arriving at Rāvan's court Hanumān scrutinized it, and its superb glory baffled all descriptions. Even the gods and the regents-of-quarters stood meekly there with hands folded, ever watchful of the mere hint of Rāvan's eyebrow in great fear. The monkey's heart remained unruffled at the sight of such power and splendor—even as a Garud remains unconcerned amidst serpents, even though countless in numbers.

जब तें रामु ब्याहि घर आए । नित नव मंगल मोद बधाए ॥
दीन दयाल बिरिदु संभारी । हरहु नाथ मम संकट भारी ॥
मंगल भवन अमंगल हारी । द्रवउ सो दसरथ अजिर बिहारी ॥

दोहा-*dohā:*

कपिहि बिलोकि दसानन बिहसा कहि दुर्बाद ।
kapihi biloki dasānana bihasā kahi durbāda;
सुत बध सुरति कीन्हि पुनि उपजा हृदयँ बिषाद ॥२०॥
suta badha surati kīnhi puni upajā hṛdayam̐ biṣāda. 20 .

प्रबिसि नगर कीजे सब काजा । हृदयँ राखि कोसलपुर राजा ॥
जपहिं नामु जन आरत भारी । मिटहिं कुसंकट होहिं सुखारी ॥
सियावर राम जय जय राम । मेरे प्रभु राम जय जय राम ॥

When he looked at the monkey, Rāvan laughed contemptuously and mocked him; then remembering his son's death his heart grew sad.

चौपाई-caupāī:

कह लंकेस कवन तैं कीसा । केहि कें बल घालेहि बन खीसा ॥
kaha laṁkesa kavana taiṁ kīsā, kehi keṁ bala ghālehi bana khīsā .
की धौं श्रवन सुनेहि नहिं मोही । देखउँ अति असंक सठ तोही ॥
kī dhauṁ śravana sunehi nahiṁ mohī, dekhauṁ ati asaṁka saṭha tohī .
मारे निसिचर केहिं अपराधा । कहु सठ तोहि न प्रान कइ बाधा ॥
māre nisicara kehiṁ aparādhā, kahu saṭha tohi na prāna kai bādhā .
सुनु रावन ब्रह्मांड निकाया । पाइ जासु बल बिरचति माया ॥
sunu rāvana brahmāṁḍa nikāyā, pāi jāsu bala biracati māyā .
जाकें बल बिरंचि हरि ईसा । पालत सृजत हरत दससीसा ॥
jākeṁ bala biraṁci hari īsā, pālata sṛjata harata dasasīsā .
जा बल सीस धरत सहसानन । अंडकोस समेत गिरि कानन ॥
jā bala sīsa dharata sahasānana, aṁḍakosa sameta giri kānana .
धरइ जो बिबिध देह सुरत्राता । तुम्ह ते सठन्ह सिखावनु दाता ॥
dharai jo bibidha deha suratrātā, tumha te saṭhanha sikhāvanu dātā .
हर कोदंड कठिन जेहिं भंजा । तेहि समेत नृप दल मद गंजा ॥
hara kodaṁḍa kaṭhina jehiṁ bhaṁjā, tehi sameta nṛpa dala mada gaṁjā.
खर दूषन त्रिसिरा अरु बाली । बधे सकल अतुलित बलसाली ॥
khara dūṣana trisirā aru bālī, badhe sakala atulita balasālī .

The King of Lankā then thundered, "Who are you monkey and by whose right have you wrought destruction on the Grove? What! Have you never heard of me and my repute? Wretch, I can see that you are exceptionally bold! For what offence did you put the guards to death? Tell me fool—are you not afraid of losing your life?" "Listen Rāvan: He—by whose power Māyā has spun out this sphere of existence—borrowing whose might, Brahmmā, Vishnu, and Īsha carry on with their respective functions of creation, preservation and destruction—by whose might again, the thousand-headed serpent supports on his pate the entire globe with its mountains and forests—who from Age to Age takes on various Avatars in order to protect the virtuous—and who, in order to teach lesson to wretches like you, broke Shiva's unbending bow and thereby crushed with it the pride of an assemblage of kings—and who slew Khara and Dushan, Trisira and Bali, all of matchless strengths;—

जब तें रामु ब्याहि घर आए । नित नव मंगल मोद बधाए ॥
दीन दयाल बिरिदु संभारी । हरहु नाथ मम संकट भारी ॥
मंगल भवन अमंगल हारी । द्रवउ सो दसरथ अजिर बिहारी ॥

दोहा-*dohā:*

जाके बल लवलेस तें जितेहु चराचर झारि ।
jāke bala lavalesa teṁ jitehu carācara jhāri,
तासु दूत मैं जा करि हरि आनेहु प्रिय नारि ॥२१॥
tāsu dūta maiṁ jā kari hari ānehu priya nāri. 21 .

प्रबिसि नगर कीजे सब काजा । हृदयँ राखि कोसलपुर राजा ॥
जपहिं नामु जन आरत भारी । मिटहिं कुसंकट होहिं सुखारी ॥
सियावर राम जय जय राम । मेरे प्रभु राम जय जय राम ॥

—and borrowing a fraction of whose strength you were able to conquer many worlds—and whose beloved spouse you have craftily abducted—it is He, Shrī Rāma, whose envoy I am.

Dt: ____________________

चौपाई-*caupāī:*

जानउँ मैं तुम्हारि प्रभुताई । सहसबाहु सन परी लराई ॥
jānauṁ maiṁ tumhāri prabhutāī, sahasabāhu sana parī larāī .
समर बालि सन करि जसु पावा । सुनि कपि बचन बिहसि बिहरावा ॥
samara bāli sana kari jasu pāvā, suni kapi bacana bihasi biharāvā .
खायउँ फल प्रभु लागी भूँखा । कपि सुभाव तें तोरेउँ रूखा ॥
khāyauṁ phala prabhu lāgī bhūṁkhā, kapi subhāva teṁ toreuṁ rūkhā .
सब कें देह परम प्रिय स्वामी । मारहिं मोहि कुमारग गामी ॥
saba keṁ deha parama priya svāmī, mārahiṁ mohi kumāraga gāmī .
जिन्ह मोहि मारा ते मैं मारे । तेहि पर बाँधेउँ तनयँ तुम्हारे ॥
jinha mohi mārā te maiṁ māre, tehi para bāṁdheṁ tanayaṁ tumhāre .
मोहि न कछु बाँधे कइ लाजा । कीन्ह चहउँ निज प्रभु कर काजा ॥
mohi na kachu bāṁdhe kai lājā, kīnha cahauṁ nija prabhu kara kājā .
बिनती करउँ जोरि कर रावन । सुनहु मान तजि मोर सिखावन ॥
binatī karauṁ jori kara rāvana, sunahu māna taji mora sikhāvana .
देखहु तुम्ह निज कुलहि बिचारी । भ्रम तजि भजहु भगत भय हारी ॥
dekhahu tumha nija kulahi bicārī, bhrama taji bhajahu bhagata bhaya hārī .
जाकें डर अति काल डेराई । जो सुर असुर चराचर खाई ॥
jākeṁ ḍara ati kāla ḍerāī, jo sura asura carācara khāī .
तासों बयरु कबहुँ नहिं कीजै । मोरे कहें जानकी दीजै ॥
tāsoṁ bayaru kabahuṁ nahiṁ kījai, more kaheṁ jānakī dījai .

And as for you, I know all your repute—for was it not you who battled with Sahastrabhuj [and lost]? And again, who doesn't know of your renown in your conflict with Bāli [who humiliated you]." At Hanumān's sarcasm, Rāvan could but put on a deceptive smile of dismissal. Hanumān spoke again, "I was hungry so I ate the fruits; and a monkey is wont to break a few boughs and trees—what of it? And when those wicked doers insisted on beating me then I had no recourse but to return blow for a blow—after all one's body, sir, is supremely dear to all. [I am blameless] and yet your son has put me in these bonds—bonds that I am in no way ashamed of—because my objective is to accomplish my master's work. Now Rāvan I implore you with folded hands—abandon your pride and tend to my advice—and do consider it very carefully in your heart: wake up from your hallucinations, and worship Shrī Rāma, who rids his devotees of every fear. He, who is feared even by Death—which itself is known to devour everything, animate & inanimate, gods & demons—do not, O Rāvan, antagonize that Supreme-Being, and do please return Jānakī at my behest.

जब तें रामु ब्याहि घर आए । नित नव मंगल मोद बधाए ॥
दीन दयाल बिरिदु संभारी । हरहु नाथ मम संकट भारी ॥
मंगल भवन अमंगल हारी । द्रवउ सो दसरथ अजिर बिहारी ॥

दोहा-*dohā:*

मोहमूल बहु सूल प्रद त्यागहु तम अभिमान ।
mohamūla bahu sūla prada tyāgahu tama abhimāna,
भजहु राम रघुनायक कृपा सिंधु भगवान ॥२३॥
bhajahu rāma raghunāyaka kṛpā siṁdhu bhagavāna. 23.

प्रबिसि नगर कीजे सब काजा । हृदयँ राखि कोसलपुर राजा ॥
जपहिं नामु जन आरत भारी । मिटहिं कुसंकट होहिं सुखारी ॥
सियावर राम जय जय राम । मेरे प्रभु राम जय जय राम ॥

Abandon arrogance—which is the embodiment of Tamas, rooted as it is in Ignorance—that fount of endless pain—and adore the Chief of Raghus, Bhagwān Rāma, the very Ocean of Compassion."

Dt: ____________________

चौपाई-*caupāī:*

जदपि कही कपि अति हित बानी । भगति बिबेक बिरति नय सानी ॥
jadapi kahī kapi ati hita bānī, bhagati bibeka birati naya sānī .
बोला बिहसि महा अभिमानी । मिला हमहि कपि गुर बड़ ग्यानी ॥
bolā bihasi mahā abhimānī, milā hamahi kapi gura baṛa gyānī .
मृत्यु निकट आई खल तोही । लागेसि अधम सिखावन मोही ॥
mṛtyu nikaṭa āī khala tohī, lāgesi adhama sikhāvana mohī .
उलटा होइहि कह हनुमाना । मतिभ्रम तोर प्रगट मैं जाना ॥
ulaṭā hoihi kaha hanumānā, matibhrama tora pragaṭa maiṁ jānā .
सुनि कपि बचन बहुत खिसिआना । बेगि न हरहु मूढ़ कर प्राना ॥
suni kapi bacana bahuta khisiānā, begi na harahu mūṛha kara prānā .
सुनत निसाचर मारन धाए । सचिवन्ह सहित बिभीषनु आए ॥
sunata nisācara mārana dhāe, sacivanha sahita bibhīṣanu āe .
नाइ सीस करि बिनय बहूता । नीति बिरोध न मारिअ दूता ॥
nāi sīsa kari binaya bahūtā, nīti birodha na māria dūtā .
आन दंड कछु करिअ गोसाँई । सबहीं कहा मंत्र भल भाई ॥
āna daṁḍa kachu karia gosāṁī, sabahīṁ kahā maṁtra bhala bhāī .
सुनत बिहसि बोला दसकंधर । अंग भंग करि पठइअ बंदर ॥
sunata bihasi bolā dasakaṁdhara, aṁga bhaṁga kari paṭhaia baṁdara .

Although the monkey spoke friendly wise and gave exceedingly salutary advice—replete with devotion, discrimination, dispassion, depth—the haughty monster-king laughed and spoke with disdain, "Ah, what a wise sage we have found today, and in a monkey at that! You dare to preach me, you fool! Wretch, you are an inch away from your death." "Actually, the very opposite is the case", retorted Hanumān, "For I clearly perceive that you have become delusional." Hearing those words, the humiliated demon-king gnashed his teeth in fury, "Quick someone, put an end to this fool's life." Obediently several monsters rushed forward to strike him. At that moment Vibhishan stepped up along with his ministers, and bowing his head made this humble petition: "It is against all rules of statecraft to slay an emissary; perhaps he can be punished some other way, O master." "That indeed is sound counsel friends", many agreed. Hearing this Rāvan laughingly said, "All right then, let the monkey go after he has been mutilated.

जब तें रामु ब्याहि घर आए । नित नव मंगल मोद बधाए ॥
दीन दयाल बिरिदु संभारी । हरहु नाथ मम संकट भारी ॥
मंगल भवन अमंगल हारी । द्रवउ सो दसरथ अजिर बिहारी ॥

दोहा-*dohā:*

कपि कें ममता पूँछ पर सबहि कहउँ समुझाइ ।
kapi kem̐ mamatā pūm̐cha para sabahi kahaum̐ samujhāi,
तेल बोरि पट बाँधि पुनि पावक देहु लगाइ ॥२४॥
tela bori paṭa bām̐dhi puni pāvaka dehu lagāi. 24 .

प्रबिसि नगर कीजे सब काजा । हृदयँ राखि कोसलपुर राजा ॥
जपहिं नामु जन आरत भारी । मिटहिं कुसंकट होहिं सुखारी ॥
सियावर राम जय जय राम । मेरे प्रभु राम जय जय राम ॥

And let me impart to you this sagacious advice: a monkey is very fond of his tail. So wrap his tail in oil-soaked rags and then set fire to it.

Dt: ______________________

चौपाई-*caupāī:*

पूँछहीन बानर तहँ जाइहि । तब सठ निज नाथहि लइ आइहि ॥
pūm̐chahīna bānara taham̐ jāihi, taba saṭha nija nāthahi lai āihi .
जिन्ह कै कीन्हिसि बहुत बड़ाई । देखउँ मैं तिन्ह कै प्रभुताई ॥
jinha kai kīnhisi bahuta baṛāī, dekhaum̐ maiṁ tinha kai prabhutāī .
बचन सुनत कपि मन मुसुकाना । भइ सहाय सारद मैं जाना ॥
bacana sunata kapi mana musukānā, bhai sahāya sārada maiṁ jānā .
जातुधान सुनि रावन बचना । लागे रचैं मूढ़ सोइ रचना ॥
jātudhāna suni rāvana bacanā, lāge racaiṁ mūṛha soi racanā .
रहा न नगर बसन घृत तेला । बाढ़ी पूँछ कीन्ह कपि खेला ॥
rahā na nagara basana ghṛta telā, bāṛhī pūm̐cha kīnha kapi khelā .
कौतुक कहँ आए पुरबासी । मारहिं चरन करहिं बहु हाँसी ॥
kautuka kaham̐ āe purabāsī, mārahiṁ carana karahiṁ bahu hām̐sī .
बाजहिं ढोल देहिं सब तारी । नगर फेरि पुनि पूँछ प्रजारी ॥
bājahiṁ ḍhola dehiṁ saba tārī, nagara pheri puni pūm̐cha prajārī .
पावक जरत देखि हनुमंता । भयउ परम लघुरुप तुरंता ॥
pāvaka jarata dekhi hanumaṁtā, bhayau parama laghurupa turaṁtā .
निबुकि चढ़ेउ कपि कनक अटारीं । भईं सभीत निसाचर नारीं ॥
nibuki caṛheu kapi kanaka aṭārīṁ, bhaīṁ sabhīta nisācara nārīṁ .

The poor tail-less wretch can then go fetch his master and I will get to see him whose powers he so lavishly extols." The monkey smiled to himself upon hearing this, 'Goddess Shārdā is certainly proving helpful it seems.' Obedient to Rāvan's command the foolish demons began to do what they were ordained. Not a rag was left in the city, nor a drop of *ghī* or oil—to such a length Hanumān grew his tail in playful gesture. The citizens throng to see the fun, and they kick him and jeer at him, and with the beating of drums and clapping of hands they parade the monkey throughout the city; and then they set fire to his tail. When Hanumān saw that the fire had been lit, he at once reduced himself to a diminutive size. Slipping out of bonds he sprang atop the attics of the gilded mansions—much to the dismay of the females of demons there.

दोहा-*dohā:*

हरि प्रेरित तेहि अवसर चले मरुत उनचास।
hari prerita tehi avasara cale maruta unacāsa,
अट्टहास करि गर्जा कपि बढ़ि लाग अकास॥२५॥
aṭṭahāsa kari garjā kapi baṛhi lāga akāsa. 25 .

Impelled by Hari's will, at that very instance, the Forty-Nine Winds began to bluster and rage. Hanumān howled and roared and swelled himself to such a size that he seemed to touch the very tips of heaven.

चौपाई-caupāī:

देह बिसाल परम हरुआई । मंदिर तें मंदिर चढ़ धाई ॥
deha bisāla parama haruāī, maṁdira teṁ maṁdira caṛha dhāī .
जरइ नगर भा लोग बिहाला । झपट लपट बहु कोटि कराला ॥
jarai nagara bhā loga bihālā, jhapaṭa lapaṭa bahu koṭi karālā .
तात मातु हा सुनिअ पुकारा । एहिं अवसर को हमहि उबारा ॥
tāta mātu hā sunia pukārā, ehiṁ avasara ko hamahi ubārā .
हम जो कहा यह कपि नहिं होई । बानर रूप धरें सुर कोई ॥
hama jo kahā yaha kapi nahiṁ hoī, bānara rūpa dhareṁ sura koī .
साधु अवग्या कर फलु ऐसा । जरइ नगर अनाथ कर जैसा ॥
sādhu avagyā kara phalu aisā, jarai nagara anātha kara jaisā .
जारा नगरु निमिष एक माहीं । एक बिभीषन कर गृह नाहीं ॥
jārā nagaru nimiṣa eka māhīṁ, eka bibhīṣana kara gṛha nāhīṁ .
ता कर दूत अनल जेहिं सिरिजा । जरा न सो तेहि कारन गिरिजा ॥
tā kara dūta anala jehiṁ sirijā, jarā na so tehi kārana girijā .
उलटि पलटि लंका सब जारी । कूदि परा पुनि सिंधु मझारी ॥
ulaṭi palaṭi laṁkā saba jārī, kūdi parā puni siṁdhu majhārī .

Of such an enormous stature, and yet so marvelously agile, Hanumān leaped about, going from one mansion to another. The city started to burn and the people became mortified and helpless as the terrible flames burst forth in countless million places everywhere. Piteous were the cries that could be heard all around: "O my father! O my mother! Help! Someone, come save us at this hour! Well did I earlier say that this is no monkey but some god in a monkey's shape." Such is the result of deriding a noble soul—the city burned in flames as though bereft and orphaned. In the twinkling of eye Hanumān burnt the whole city down barring the solitary mansion of Vibhishan. O Girijā [says Shiva], Hanumān is the emissary of Rāma—He who created the element of Fire itself, so it is no wonder that Hanumān himself remained unscathed. Turning the entirety of Lankā upside down—burning it from one end to other—Hanumān then leapt into the sea.

जब तें रामु ब्याहि घर आए । नित नव मंगल मोद बधाए ॥
दीन दयाल बिरिदु संभारी । हरहु नाथ मम संकट भारी ॥
मंगल भवन अमंगल हारी । द्रवउ सो दसरथ अजिर बिहारी ॥

प्रबिसि नगर कीजे सब काजा । हृदयँ राखि कोसलपुर राजा ॥
जपहिं नामु जन आरत भारी । मिटहिं कुसंकट होहिं सुखारी ॥
सियावर राम जय जय राम । मेरे प्रभु राम जय जय राम ॥

दोहा-dohā:

पूँछ बुझाइ खोइ श्रम धरि लघु रूप बहोरि ।
pūm̐cha bujhāi khoi śrama dhari laghu rūpa bahori,
जनकसुता कें आगें ठाढ़ भयउ कर जोरि ॥२६॥
janakasutā keṁ āgeṁ ṭhāṛha bhayau kara jori. 26 .

After dousing the flames on the tail and having recuperated from his fatigue, Hanumān assumed the diminutive form and went and stood before mother Jānakī, his hands clasped in prayer.

चौपाई-*caupāī:*

मातु मोहि दीजे कछु चीन्हा । जैसें रघुनायक मोहि दीन्हा ॥
mātu mohi dīje kachu cīnhā, jaisem̐ raghunāyaka mohi dīnhā .
चूड़ामनि उतारि तब दयऊ । हरष समेत पवनसुत लयऊ ॥
cūṛāmani utāri taba dayaū, haraṣa sameta pavanasuta layaū .
कहेहु तात अस मोर प्रनामा । सब प्रकार प्रभु पूरनकामा ॥
kahehu tāta asa mora pranāmā, saba prakāra prabhu pūranakāmā .
दीन दयाल बिरिदु संभारी । हरहु नाथ मम संकट भारी ॥
dīna dayāla biridu saṁbhārī, harahu nātha mama saṁkaṭa bhārī .
तात सक्रसुत कथा सुनाएहु । बान प्रताप प्रभुहि समुझाएहु ॥
tāta sakrasuta kathā sunāehu, bāna pratāpa prabhuhi samujhāehu .
मास दिवस महुँ नाथु न आवा । तौ पुनि मोहि जिअत नहिं पावा ॥
māsa divasa mahum̐ nāthu na āvā, tau puni mohi jiata nahiṁ pāvā .
कहु कपि केहि बिधि राखौं प्राना । तुम्हहू तात कहत अब जाना ॥
kahu kapi kehi bidhi rākhauṁ prānā, tumhahū tāta kahata aba jānā .
तोहि देखि सीतलि भइ छाती । पुनि मो कहुँ सोइ दिनु सो राती ॥
tohi dekhi sītali bhai chātī, puni mo kahum̐ soi dinu so rātī .

"Be pleased, O mother, to give me some token such as Raghunāyak gave me." Thereupon Sītā unfastened the crest-jewel from her hair and gave it to him; and the son-of-wind received it with great joy. "Convey my obeisance to him, dear son, and recite to him my prayer: 'You, my Lord, are all-sufficient, and it is your wont to be most genial to the distressed—you yourself have so avowed and bind yourself to that repute. Now relieve me, O Lord, from this most grievous affliction.' Repeat to him, son, the story of Indra's son, and remind my Lord of the might of his arrows. If the Lord does not arrive within a month's time, he will not find me in this body again. Tell me O Kapi, how I can preserve my life, for you too now talk of leaving? Your sight had brought some relief to my heavy heart, but I now have before me the same dreadful days and nights."

जब तें रामु ब्याहि घर आए । नित नव मंगल मोद बधाए ॥
दीन दयाल बिरिदु संभारी । हरहु नाथ मम संकट भारी ॥
मंगल भवन अमंगल हारी । द्रवउ सो दसरथ अजिर बिहारी ॥

दोहा-*dohā:*

जनकसुतहि समुझाइ करि बहु बिधि धीरजु दीन्ह ।
janakasutahi samujhāi kari bahu bidhi dhīraju dīnha,
चरन कमल सिरु नाइ कपि गवनु राम पहिं कीन्ह ॥२७॥
carana kamala siru nāi kapi gavanu rāma pahiṁ kīnha. 27.

प्रबिसि नगर कीजे सब काजा । हृदयँ राखि कोसलपुर राजा ॥
जपहिं नामु जन आरत भारी । मिटहिं कुसंकट होहिं सुखारी ॥
सियावर राम जय जय राम । मेरे प्रभु राम जय जय राम ॥

Consoling her with many words Hanumān did everything he could to inspire confidence in Janak's daughter; then bowing his head at her lotus feet, Hanumān sallied forth to rejoin Shrī Rāma.

चौपाई-*caupāī:*

चलत महाधुनि गर्जेसि भारी । गर्भ स्रवहिं सुनि निसिचर नारी ॥
calata mahādhuni garjesi bhārī, garbha sravahiṁ suni nisicara nārī .
नाघि सिंधु एहि पारहि आवा । सबद किलिकिला कपिन्ह सुनावा ॥
nāghi siṁdhu ehi pārahi āvā, sabada kilikilā kapinha sunāvā .
हरषे सब बिलोकि हनुमाना । नूतन जन्म कपिन्ह तब जाना ॥
haraṣe saba biloki hanumānā, nūtana janma kapinha taba jānā .
मुख प्रसन्न तन तेज बिराजा । कीन्हेसि रामचन्द्र कर काजा ॥
mukha prasanna tana teja birājā, kīnhesi rāmacandra kara kājā .
मिले सकल अति भए सुखारी । तलफत मीन पाव जिमि बारी ॥
mile sakala ati bhae sukhārī, talaphata mīna pāva jimi bārī .
चले हरषि रघुनायक पासा । पूँछत कहत नवल इतिहासा ॥
cale haraṣi raghunāyaka pāsā, pūm̐chata kahata navala itihāsā .
तब मधुबन भीतर सब आए । अंगद संमत मधु फल खाए ॥
taba madhubana bhītara saba āe, aṁgada saṁmata madhu phala khāe .
रखवारे जब बरजन लागे । मुष्टि प्रहार हनत सब भागे ॥
rakhavāre jaba barajana lāge, muṣṭi prahāra hanata saba bhāge .

As he left he bellowed terribly—letting out a horrendous roar, a sound so frightful that some wives of demons were seized with premature childbirths upon hearing that. Leaping across the sea Hanumān arrived on the other side and made a loud clarion sound of victory for the monkeys to hear—who became exceedingly overjoyed at the sight, as if given a new spell of life. Hanumān wore a most cheerful countenance and his body glistened with brilliant resplendency. The monkeys were left in no doubt that Hanumān had accomplished the mission of Shrī Rāma. Supremely thrilled, they all eagerly greeted Hanumān—it was as if a fish writhing with agony on ground had found the waters again. Joyfully now they commenced their return journey to Raghunāth—on the way repeatedly asking Hanumān to relate everything which had transpired at Lankā. Reaching the Madhuban garden—and obtaining prince Aṁgad's consent—they began eating the delicious fruits from the trees there. The guards tried to stop them but, beaten off with fisticuffs, they took to their heels.

दोहा-dohā:

जाइ पुकारे ते सब बन उजार जुबराज ।
jāi pukāre te saba bana ujāra jubarāja,
सुनि सुग्रीव हरष कपि करि आए प्रभु काज ॥२८॥
suni sugrīva haraṣa kapi kari āe prabhu kāja. 28 .

Approaching Sugrīv the guards complained that the crown-prince was laying waste to the royal garden. Sugrīv greatly rejoiced to hear that: 'Surely the monkey must have successfully completed the mission of the Lord', he thought.

चौपाई-*caupāī:*

जौं न होति सीता सुधि पाई । मधुबन के फल सकहिं कि खाई ॥
jaum̐ na hoti sītā sudhi pāī, madhubana ke phala sakahim̐ ki khāī .
एहि बिधि मन बिचार कर राजा । आइ गए कपि सहित समाजा ॥
ehi bidhi mana bicāra kara rājā, āi gae kapi sahita samājā .
आइ सबन्हि नावा पद सीसा । मिलेउ सबन्हि अति प्रेम कपीसा ॥
āi sabanhi nāvā pada sīsā, mileu sabanhi ati prema kapīsā .
पूँछी कुसल कुसल पद देखी । राम कृपाँ भा काजु बिसेषी ॥
pūm̐chī kusala kusala pada dekhī, rāma kṛpām̐ bhā kāju biseṣī .
नाथ काजु कीन्हेउ हनुमाना । राखे सकल कपिन्ह के प्राना ॥
nātha kāju kīnheu hanumānā, rākhe sakala kapinha ke prānā .
सुनि सुग्रीव बहुरि तेहि मिलेऊ । कपिन्ह सहित रघुपति पहिं चलेऊ ॥
suni sugrīva bahuri tehi mileū, kapinha sahita raghupati pahim̐ caleū .
राम कपिन्ह जब आवत देखा । किएँ काजु मन हरष बिसेषा ॥
rāma kapinha jaba āvata dekhā, kiem̐ kāju mana haraṣa biseṣā .
फटिक सिला बैठे द्वौ भाई । परे सकल कपि चरनन्हि जाई ॥
phaṭika silā baiṭhe dvau bhāī, pare sakala kapi carananhi jāī .

'For if they had failed to get any news of Sītā, they wouldn't have dared pluck the Madhuban fruits.' While the king was thus reasoning, the troops arrived there along with their chiefs. Drawing near they bowed their heads at his feet, and the king of monkeys received them most lovingly, enquiring after their welfare. "It is well with us, now that we have seen your feet. By the grace of Shri Rāma, the mission has been accomplished with remarkable success. It is Hanumān, your majesty, who achieved everything and saved the life of all of us." Hearing this Sugrīv embraced Hanumān once again, and all the monkeys then proceeded to go meet the Lord of the Raghus. When Rāma saw them coming he felt a great joy and knew that they had succeeded. The two brothers were seated on a large crystal rock and the monkeys went and prostrated at their holy feet.

जब तें रामु ब्याहि घर आए । नित नव मंगल मोद बधाए ॥
दीन दयाल बिरिदु संभारी । हरहु नाथ मम संकट भारी ॥
मंगल भवन अमंगल हारी । द्रवउ सो दसरथ अजिर बिहारी ॥

दोहा-*dohā:*

प्रीति सहित सब भेटे रघुपति करुना पुंज ।
prīti sahita saba bheṭe raghupati karunā puṁja,
पूँछी कुसल नाथ अब कुसल देखि पद कंज ॥२९॥
pūm̐chī kusala nātha aba kusala dekhi pada kaṁja. 29 .

प्रबिसि नगर कीजे सब काजा । हृदयँ राखि कोसलपुर राजा ॥
जपहिं नामु जन आरत भारी । मिटहिं कुसंकट होहिं सुखारी ॥
सियावर राम जय जय राम । मेरे प्रभु राम जय जय राम ॥

Raghupati, the ocean of infinite tenderness, greeted them with great affection and asked of their welfare. “All is well with us, O Lord, now that we have seen your lotus feet.”

चौपाई-*caupāī:*

जामवंत कह सुनु रघुराया । जा पर नाथ करहु तुम्ह दाया ॥
jāmavaṁta kaha sunu raghurāyā, jā para nātha karahu tumha dāyā .
ताहि सदा सुभ कुसल निरंतर । सुर नर मुनि प्रसन्न ता ऊपर ॥
tāhi sadā subha kusala niraṁtara, sura nara muni prasanna tā ūpara .
सोइ बिजई बिनई गुन सागर । तासु सुजसु त्रैलोक उजागर ॥
soi bijaī binaī guna sāgara, tāsu sujasu trailoka ujāgara .
प्रभु कीं कृपा भयउ सबु काजू । जन्म हमार सुफल भा आजू ॥
prabhu kīṁ kṛpā bhayau sabu kājū, janma hamāra suphala bhā ājū .
नाथ पवनसुत कीन्हि जो करनी । सहसहुँ मुख न जाइ सो बरनी ॥
nātha pavanasuta kīnhi jo karanī, sahasahum̐ mukha na jāi so baranī .
पवनतनय के चरित सुहाए । जामवंत रघुपतिहि सुनाए ॥
pavanatanaya ke carita suhāe, jāmavaṁta raghupatihi sunāe .
सुनत कृपानिधि मन अति भाए । पुनि हनुमान हरषि हियँ लाए ॥
sunata kṛpānidhi mana ati bhāe, puni hanumāna haraṣi hiyam̐ lāe .
कहहु तात केहि भाँति जानकी । रहति करति रच्छा स्वप्रान की ॥
kahahu tāta kehi bhām̐ti jānakī, rahati karati racchā svaprāna kī .

Said Jāmavaṁt, "Hearken, O Raghurai: upon whom you bestow your favor—they become ever auspicious, ever felicitous, ever fortunate; and unto them gods, men and saints remain ever gracious. They whom you bless, become modest, oceans of virtues, and ever victorious; and their fair renown irradiates through all the spheres of creation. By the favor of you, my Lord, the task was admirably accomplished and today we can say that our birth here on earth has been rendered worthy. And Lord, to speak of all of Hanumān's doings would be too much for even a thousand tongues." Jāmavaṁt then narrated to Raghupati the enchanting exploits of the son-of-wind. The All-merciful became spellbound hearing the recital of Hanumān's enactments and clasped Hanumān to his heart with great joy. "Tell me O son, how abides Jānakī? How is she able to preserve her life?"

दोहा-dohā:

नाम पाहरु दिवस निसि ध्यान तुम्हार कपाट ।

nāma pāharu divasa nisi dhyāna tumhāra kapāṭa,

लोचन निज पद जंत्रित जाहिं प्रान केहिं बाट ॥३०॥

locana nija pada jaṁtrita jāhiṁ prāna kehiṁ bāṭa. 30 .

“Her continual thought of you, my Lord, is the barred door; and your Name is the sentinel that keeps watch over her by day and by night; and her feet are held fast by her eyes which are always looking down upon them; and thus there is no outlet whereby her life may walk, escape, flit away, leave!

जब तें रामु ब्याहि घर आए। नित नव मंगल मोद बधाए॥
दीन दयाल बिरिदु संभारी। हरहु नाथ मम संकट भारी॥
मंगल भवन अमंगल हारी। द्रवउ सो दसरथ अजिर बिहारी॥

प्रबिसि नगर कीजे सब काजा। हृदयँ राखि कोसलपुर राजा॥
जपहिं नामु जन आरत भारी। मिटहिं कुसंकट होहिं सुखारी॥
सियावर राम जय जय राम। मेरे प्रभु राम जय जय राम॥

चौपाई-*caupāī:*

चलत मोहि चूडामनि दीन्ही । रघुपति हृदयँ लाइ सोइ लीन्ही ॥
calata mohi cūṛāmani dīnhī, raghupati hṛdayam̐ lāi soi līnhī .
नाथ जुगल लोचन भरि बारी । बचन कहे कछु जनककुमारी ॥
nātha jugala locana bhari bārī, bacana kahe kachu janakakumārī .
अनुज समेत गहेहु प्रभु चरना । दीन बंधु प्रनतारति हरना ॥
anuja sameta gahehu prabhu caranā, dīna baṁdhu pranatārati haranā .
मन क्रम बचन चरन अनुरागी । केहिं अपराध नाथ हौं त्यागी ॥
mana krama bacana carana anurāgī, kehiṁ aparādha nātha hauṁ tyāgī .
अवगुन एक मोर मैं माना । बिछुरत प्रान न कीन्ह पयाना ॥
avaguna eka mora maiṁ mānā, bichurata prāna na kīnha payānā .
नाथ सो नयनन्हि को अपराधा । निसरत प्रान करहिं हठि बाधा ॥
nātha so nayananhi ko aparādhā, nisarata prāna karahiṁ haṭhi bādhā .
बिरह अगिनि तनु तूल समीरा । स्वास जरइ छन माहिं सरीरा ॥
biraha agini tanu tūla samīrā, svāsa jarai chana māhiṁ sarīrā .
नयन स्त्रवहिं जलु निज हित लागी । जरैं न पाव देह बिरहागी ॥
nayana sravahiṁ jalu nija hita lāgī, jaraiṁ na pāva deha birahāgī .
सीता कै अति बिपति बिसाला । बिनहिं कहें भलि दीनदयाला ॥
sītā kai ati bipati bisālā, binahiṁ kaheṁ bhali dīnadayālā .

When I was leaving, she gave me this crest-jewel from her hair." Raghupati took it and clasped it to his heart. "And my lord, with her eyes overflowing with tears the daughter of Janak spake these words: Embrace the feet of my lord along with his brother, crying, "O friend of the poor, O reliever of the supplicant's distress! In heart, word, and deed, I am consecrated to your service; for what offence then, my lord, have you forsaken me? I do admit to this one fault of mine: that my life did not at once part, the moment I was, from you, ripped apart. But this, my Lord, is the fault of these eyes, which perforce prevent my soul from taking flight. The agony of separation from you is like a fire; and my sighs fan it as gusts of wind; and there stands my body like a heap of cotton—which should have been consumed in an instant but for these eyes. My eyes, in their selfishness—to once again behold your beautiful form—rain down flood of tears; and that is why my body fails to burn even through this intense fire of bereavement." Sītā's suffering is so overwhelmingly great, and you are so compassionate to the afflicted, O Lord, that I would fain not describe her distress any further.

दोहा-*dohā:*

निमिष निमिष करुनानिधि जाहिं कलप सम बीति ।
nimiṣa nimiṣa karunānidhi jāhiṁ kalapa sama bīti,
बेगि चलिय प्रभु आनिअ भुज बल खल दल जीति ॥३१॥
begi caliya prabhu ānia bhuja bala khala dala jīti. 31 .

Each and every single moment for her, passes like an Age, O fount of mercy. So set out with haste, my Lord, and vanquish that army of reprobates by the might of your great arms."

चौपाई-*caupāī:*

सुनि सीता दुख प्रभु सुख अयना । भरि आए जल राजिव नयना ॥
suni sītā dukha prabhu sukha ayanā, bhari āe jala rājiva nayanā .
बचन कायँ मन मम गति जाही । सपनेहुँ बूझिअ बिपति कि ताही ॥
bacana kāyam̐ mana mama gati jāhī, sapanehum̐ būjhia bipati ki tāhī .
कह हनुमंत बिपति प्रभु सोई । जब तव सुमिरन भजन न होई ॥
kaha hanumaṁta bipati prabhu soī, jaba tava sumirana bhajana na hoī .
केतिक बात प्रभु जातुधान की । रिपुहि जीति आनिबी जानकी ॥
ketika bāta prabhu jātudhāna kī, ripuhi jīti ānibī jānakī .
सुनु कपि तोहि समान उपकारी । नहिं कोउ सुर नर मुनि तनुधारी ॥
sunu kapi tohi samāna upakārī, nahiṁ kou sura nara muni tanudhārī .
प्रति उपकार करौं का तोरा । सनमुख होइ न सकत मन मोरा ॥
prati upakāra karauṁ kā torā, sanamukha hoi na sakata mana morā .
सुनु सुत तोहि उरिन मैं नाहीं । देखेउँ करि बिचार मन माहीं ॥
sunu suta tohi urina maiṁ nāhīṁ, dekheum̐ kari bicāra mana māhīṁ .
पुनि पुनि कपिहि चितव सुरत्राता । लोचन नीर पुलक अति गाता ॥
puni puni kapihi citava suratrātā, locana nīra pulaka ati gātā .

Upon hearing of Sītā's sorrows, the lotus eyes of Lord, the abode of bliss, overflowed with tears. "Can anyone—who completely depends upon me alone, in thought, word, and deed—even in dream know of adversity?" Hanumān said, "There is only one misfortune my Lord—to forget you and the devotion towards you. Of what account are these demons to my Lord, who can rout them instantly to bring Jānakī back." Then said Rāma, "Hearken O Hanumān: neither god, nor man, nor a saint exists in this world, who has been such a benefactor to me as you yourself. What return can I make unto you? There is none that occurs to my mind. Listen, my son: I have thought over this question and concluded that the debt which I owe to you can never be repaid." Again and again, as the Protector of the gods gazed upon him, Hanumān's eyes became filled with tears, and his body was overpowered with a thrill of emotion.

जब तें रामु ब्याहि घर आए । नित नव मंगल मोद बधाए ॥
दीन दयाल बिरिदु संभारी । हरहु नाथ मम संकट भारी ॥
मंगल भवन अमंगल हारी । द्रवउ सो दसरथ अजिर बिहारी ॥

दोहा-*dohā:*

सुनि प्रभु बचन बिलोकि मुख गात हरषि हनुमंत ।
suni prabhu bacana biloki mukha gāta harasi hanumaṁta;
चरन परेउ प्रेमाकुल त्राहि त्राहि भगवंत ॥३२॥
carana pareu premākula trāhi trāhi bhagavaṁta. 32 .

प्रबिसि नगर कीजे सब काजा । हृदयँ राखि कोसलपुर राजा ॥
जपहिं नामु जन आरत भारी । मिटहिं कुसंकट होहिं सुखारी ॥
सियावर राम जय जय राम । मेरे प्रभु राम जय जय राम ॥

As he listened to his Lord's words and looked upon his face, Hanumān went into rapture; and in an ecstasy of love fell down at the Lord's feet, crying, "O save me, save me, Lord-God [lest I become vainglorious]."

Dt: ______________________

चौपाई-*caupāī:*

बार बार प्रभु चहइ उठावा । प्रेम मगन तेहि उठब न भावा ॥
bāra bāra prabhu cahai uṭhāvā, prema magana tehi uṭhaba na bhāvā .
प्रभु कर पंकज कपि कें सीसा । सुमिरि सो दसा मगन गौरीसा ॥
prabhu kara paṁkaja kapi keṁ sīsā, sumiri so dasā magana gaurīsā .
सावधान मन करि पुनि संकर । लागे कहन कथा अति सुंदर ॥
sāvadhāna mana kari puni saṁkara, lāge kahana kathā ati suṁdara .
कपि उठाइ प्रभु हृदयँ लगावा । कर गहि परम निकट बैठावा ॥
kapi uṭhāi prabhu hṛdayaṁ lagāvā, kara gahi parama nikaṭa baiṭhāvā .
कहु कपि रावन पालित लंका । केहि बिधि दहेउ दुर्ग अति बंका ॥
kahu kapi rāvana pālita laṁkā, kehi bidhi daheu durga ati baṁkā .
प्रभु प्रसन्न जाना हनुमाना । बोला बचन बिगत अभिमाना ॥
prabhu prasanna jānā hanumānā, bolā bacana bigata abhimānā .
साखामृग कै बड़ि मनुसाई । साखा तें साखा पर जाई ॥
sākhāmṛga kai baṛi manusāī, sākhā teṁ sākhā para jāī .
नाघि सिंधु हाटकपुर जारा । निसिचर गन बधि बिपिन उजारा ॥
nāghi siṁdhu hāṭakapura jārā, nisicara gana badhi bipina ujārā .
सो सब तव प्रताप रघुराई । नाथ न कछू मोरि प्रभुताई ॥
so saba tava pratāpa raghurāī, nātha na kachū mori prabhutāī .

Again and again the Lord sought to raise him, but Hanumān was so overwhelmed with ecstasy that he could not rise. As he recalled to his mind—the image of the Lord and his lotus hands placed upon the monkey's head—Siva himself became overcome with emotion; but then restraining his feelings, he proceeded with the charming narrative. Rāma lifted Hanumān up and clasped him to his heart. Then he took him by the hand and seated him close to his side. "Tell me, O Kapi, by what means could you burn down the most impregnable fortress of Lankā protected by Rāvan?" The Lord is pleased, knew Hanumān; then in words altogether bereft of pride he said, "A monkey forsooth is a creature of one singular prowess, O lord—to skip about from one bough to another. That I could leap across the ocean, burn down the golden city, kill the demon hosts, and lay waste to the Ashoka-grove—it was all by dint of Your might, my Lord; no credit is due me for any of these acts.

दोहा-dohā:

ता कहुँ प्रभु कछु अगम नहिं जा पर तुम्ह अनुकूल।
tā kahum̐ prabhu kachu agama nahiṁ jā para tumha anukūla,
तव प्रभावँ बड़वानलहि जारि सकइ खलु तूल॥३३॥
tava prabhāvam̐ baṛavānalahi jāri sakai khalu tūla. 33 .

There is nothing unattainable for him upon whom you are propitious, my Lord. A mere flock of cotton—if it was your pleasure—would consume an entire volcanic fire. [The impossible becomes possible.]

चौपाई-*caupāī:*

नाथ भगति अति सुखदायनी । देहु कृपा करि अनपायनी ॥
nātha bhagati ati sukhadāyanī, dehu kṛpā kari anapāyanī .
सुनि प्रभु परम सरल कपि बानी । एवमस्तु तब कहेउ भवानी ॥
suni prabhu parama sarala kapi bānī, evamastu taba kaheu bhavānī .
उमा राम सुभाउ जेहिं जाना । ताहि भजनु तजि भाव न आना ॥
umā rāma subhāu jehiṁ jānā, tāhi bhajanu taji bhāva na ānā .
यह संबाद जासु उर आवा । रघुपति चरन भगति सोइ पावा ॥
yaha saṁbāda jāsu ura āvā, raghupati carana bhagati soi pāvā .
सुनि प्रभु बचन कहहिं कपिबृंदा । जय जय जय कृपाल सुखकंदा ॥
suni prabhu bacana kahahiṁ kapibṛṁdā, jaya jaya jaya kṛpāla sukhakaṁdā.
तब रघुपति कपिपतिहि बोलावा । कहा चलैं कर करहु बनावा ॥
taba raghupati kapipatihi bolāvā, kahā calaiṁ kara karahu banāvā .
अब बिलंबु केहि कारन कीजे । तुरत कपिन्ह कहुँ आयसु दीजे ॥
aba bilaṁbu kehi kārana kīje, turata kapinha kahuṁ āyasu dīje .
कौतुक देखि सुमन बहु बरषी । नभ तें भवन चले सुर हरषी ॥
kautuka dekhi sumana bahu baraṣī, nabha teṁ bhavana cale sura haraṣī .

Therefore, be pleased to grant to me the one and only source of supreme bliss—an unceasing Devotion to You." The Lord, O Bhavānī, heard this most guileless speech of Hanumān and ordained, "Let that come to pass!" Listen Umā, he who has come to know the true nature of Rāma, can have relish for nothing else but Devotion to Rāma. Even he, who commits this dialogue to heart, gets blessed with devotion to the Lord's feet. Upon hearing the words of the Lord the monkey host applauded, "Glory, glory, all glory to the gracious Lord, the fount of bliss!" Raghupati then summoned the monkey-king and told him to make preparations for the march. "What cause is there for any delay now? Issue orders to the monkeys at once." The gods who had witnessed this spectacle rained down heaps of flowers from the skies and returned to their celestial spheres full of joy.

जब तें रामु ब्याहि घर आए । नित नव मंगल मोद बधाए ॥
दीन दयाल बिरिदु संभारी । हरहु नाथ मम संकट भारी ॥
मंगल भवन अमंगल हारी । द्रवउ सो दसरथ अजिर बिहारी ॥

दोहा-*dohā:*

कपिपति बेगि बोलाए आए जूथप जूथ ।
kapipati begi bolāe āe jūthapa jūtha,
नाना बरन अतुल बल बानर भालु बरूथ ॥३४॥
nānā barana atula bala bānara bhālu barūtha. 34 .

प्रबिसि नगर कीजे सब काजा । हृदयँ राखि कोसलपुर राजा ॥
जपहिं नामु जन आरत भारी । मिटहिं कुसंकट होहिं सुखारी ॥
सियावर राम जय जय राम । मेरे प्रभु राम जय जय राम ॥

The king of monkeys now quickly summoned the commanders and they came with their troops, presenting themselves in many ranks. Monkeys and bears, of a myriad varied hues and shapes—valiant warriors of immeasurable strength—assembled there by the multitudes.

Dt: ______________________

चौपाई-*caupāī:*

प्रभु पद पंकज नावहिं सीसा । गर्जहिं भालु महाबल कीसा ॥
prabhu pada paṁkaja nāvahiṁ sīsā, garjahiṁ bhālu mahābala kīsā .
देखी राम सकल कपि सेना । चितइ कृपा करि राजिव नैना ॥
dekhī rāma sakala kapi senā, citai kṛpā kari rājiva nainā .
राम कृपा बल पाइ कपिंदा । भए पच्छजुत मनहुँ गिरिंदा ॥
rāma kṛpā bala pāi kapiṁdā, bhae pacchajuta manahuṁ giriṁdā .
हरषि राम तब कीन्ह पयाना । सगुन भए सुंदर सुभ नाना ॥
haraṣi rāma taba kīnha payānā, saguna bhae suṁdara subha nānā .
जासु सकल मंगलमय कीती । तासु पयान सगुन यह नीती ॥
jāsu sakala maṁgalamaya kītī, tāsu payāna saguna yaha nītī .
प्रभु पयान जाना बैदेहीं । फरकि बाम अँग जनु कहि देहीं ॥
prabhu payāna jānā baidehīṁ, pharaki bāma aṁga janu kahi dehīṁ .
जोइ जोइ सगुन जानकिहि होई । असगुन भयउ रावनहि सोई ॥
joi joi saguna jānakihi hoī, asaguna bhayau rāvanahi soī .
चला कटकु को बरनैं पारा । गर्जहिं बानर भालु अपारा ॥
calā kaṭaku ko baranaiṁ pārā, garjahiṁ bānara bhālu apārā .
नख आयुध गिरि पादपधारी । चले गगन महि इच्छाचारी ॥
nakha āyudha giri pādapadhārī, cale gagana mahi icchācārī .
केहरिनाद भालु कपि करहीं । डगमगाहिं दिग्गज चिक्करहीं ॥
keharināda bhālu kapi karahīṁ, ḍagamagāhiṁ diggaja cikkarahīṁ .

They bow their heads at the Lord's lotus feet, and they roar—these thundering bears and monkeys of gigantic forms. Rāma surveyed the assembled army and cast a benign glance of gracious lotus-eyes upon them. Emboldened by his grace the monkeys appeared as like huge mountains equipped with wings. With great joy Lord Rāma then sallied forth. And many were the glad auspicious omens which occurred at that time. It was in the fitness of things that good omens should make their appearance at the time of Rāma's commencement journey—being that Rāma himself is the embodiment all auspiciousness and blessings. Over there, Videhī came to know that Rāma had embarked upon his march—for her left side throbbed as if to tell her that her Lord was coming. And every good omen which befell Jānakī was likewise altered into a bad-omen that foreboded ill for Rāvan. Now who could adequately describe the army as it rolled across the land—with countless bears and monkeys hollering terribly and loud? How they marched—brandishing trees and rocks, and with only their talons as their weapons. And as they fancied, so they moved—now flying through the air, and now speeding on the ground; and they bellowed mightily as a million lions; and with their swagger the earth quaked; and the elephants of the eight quarters trembled and they swayed.

जब तें रामु ब्याहि घर आए । नित नव मंगल मोद बधाए ॥
दीन दयाल बिरिदु संभारी । हरहु नाथ मम संकट भारी ॥
मंगल भवन अमंगल हारी । द्रवउ सो दसरथ अजिर बिहारी ॥

प्रबिसि नगर कीजे सब काजा । हृदयँ राखि कोसलपुर राजा ॥
जपहिं नामु जन आरत भारी । मिटहिं कुसंकट होहिं सुखारी ॥
सियावर राम जय जय राम । मेरे प्रभु राम जय जय राम ॥

छंद-*chaṁda:*

चिक्करहिं दिग्गज डोल महि गिरि लोल सागर खरभरे ।
cikkarahiṁ diggaja ḍola mahi giri lola sāgara kharabhare,
मन हरष सभ गंधर्ब सुर मुनि नाग किंनर दुख टरे ॥
mana haraṣa sabha gaṁdharba sura muni nāga kiṁnara dukha ṭare.
कटकटहिं मर्कट बिकट भट बहु कोटि कोटिन्ह धावहीं ।
kaṭakaṭahiṁ markaṭa bikaṭa bhaṭa bahu koṭi koṭinha dhāvahīṁ,
जय राम प्रबल प्रताप कोसलनाथ गुन गन गावहीं ॥ १ ॥
jaya rāma prabala pratāpa kosalanātha guna gana gāvahīṁ. 1 .

The guarding elephants of the eight cardinal points trumpeted and yawled; and the earth reeled and it rocked; and the mountains quivered and quaked; and the oceans stirred and raged. The sun and the moon, gods, saints, Nāgas, and Kinnars, all rejoiced in the knowledge that now our troubles will be over soon. Myriads upon myriads of enormous monkeys—warriors bellicose and belligerent, snarling and gnashing their teeth—rush onwards cheering, 'Jai Shrī Rāma'; and they shout, 'Glory to Kaushal's Lord of mighty valor'; and they hymn the praises of the Lord in a countless million ways.

सहि सक न भार उदार अहिपति बार बारहिं मोहई ।
ṣahi saka na bhāra udāra ahipati bāra bārahiṁ mohaī,
गह दसन पुनि पुनि कमठ पृष्ट कठोर सो किमि सोहई ॥
gaha dasana puni puni kamaṭha pṛṣṭa kaṭhora so kimi sohaī .
रघुबीर रुचिर प्रयान प्रस्थिति जानि परम सुहावनी ।
raghubīra rucira prayāna prasthiti jāni parama suhāvanī,
जनु कमठ खर्पर सर्पराज सो लिखत अबिचल पावनी ॥ २ ॥
janu kamaṭha kharpara sarparāja so likhata abicala pāvanī: 2 .

Even Shesha, the great lord of serpents, found himself unable to bear the crushing weight of the belligerent troops and felt dizzy again and again; and each time he would steady himself by clutching his teeth on the hard shell of the divine Tortoise. Verily the serpent-king was inscribing on the tortoise's back the saga of the hallowed glorious expedition of Shrī Rāma—knowing it to be most enchanting immortal theme for all times to come.

जब तें रामु ब्याहि घर आए । नित नव मंगल मोद बधाए ॥
दीन दयाल बिरिदु संभारी । हरहु नाथ मम संकट भारी ॥
मंगल भवन अमंगल हारी । द्रवउ सो दसरथ अजिर बिहारी ॥

दोहा-*dohā:*

एहिं बिधि जाइ कृपानिधि उतरे सागर तीर ।
ehi bidhi jāi kr̥pānidhi utare sāgara tīra,
जहँ तहँ लागे खान फल भालु बिपुल कपि बीर ॥३५॥
jahaṁ tahaṁ lāge khāna phala bhālu bipula kapi bīra. 35 .

प्रबिसि नगर कीजे सब काजा । हृदयँ राखि कोसलपुर राजा ॥
जपहिं नामु जन आरत भारी । मिटहिं कुसंकट होहिं सुखारी ॥
सियावर राम जय जय राम । मेरे प्रभु राम जय जय राम ॥

Continuing the march in this way, the All-merciful arrived at the seashore opposite Lankā and there they made their halt; the troops of valiant bears and monkeys went hither hither and thither and had their fill on fruits.

Dt.: ____________________

चौपाई-*caupāī:*

उहाँ निसाचर रहहिं ससंका । जब तें जारि गयउ कपि लंका ॥
uhām̐ nisācara rahahiṁ sasaṁkā, jaba teṁ jāri gayau kapi laṁkā .
निज निज गृहँ सब करहिं बिचारा । नहिं निसिचर कुल केर उबारा ॥
nija nija gṛham̐ saba karahiṁ bicārā, nahiṁ nisicara kula kera ubārā .
जासु दूत बल बरनि न जाई । तेहि आएँ पुर कवन भलाई ॥
jāsu dūta bala barani na jāī, tehi āem̐ pura kavana bhalāī .
दूतिन्ह सन सुनि पुरजन बानी । मंदोदरी अधिक अकुलानी ॥
dūtinha sana suni purajana bānī, maṁdodarī adhika akulānī .
रहसि जोरि कर पति पग लागी । बोली बचन नीति रस पागी ॥
rahasi jori kara pati paga lāgī, bolī bacana nīti rasa pāgī .
कंत करष हरि सन परिहरहू । मोर कहा अति हित हियँ धरहू ॥
kaṁta karaṣa hari sana pariharahū, mora kahā ati hita hiyam̐ dharahū .
समुझत जासु दूत कइ करनी । स्त्रवहिं गर्भ रजनीचर धरनी ॥
samujhata jāsu dūta kai karanī, sravahiṁ garbha rajanīcara dharanī .
तासु नारि निज सचिव बोलाई । पठवहु कंत जो चहहु भलाई ॥
tāsu nāri nija saciva bolāī, paṭhavahu kaṁta jo cahahu bhalāī .
तव कुल कमल बिपिन दुखदाई । सीता सीत निसा सम आई ॥
tava kula kamala bipina dukhadāī, sītā sīta nisā sama āī .
सुनहु नाथ सीता बिनु दीन्हें । हित न तुम्हार संभु अज कीन्हें ॥
sunahu nātha sītā binu dīnheṁ, hita na tumhāra saṁbhu aja kīnheṁ .

On the other side, the demons had been living in great fear ever since Hanumān left after burning the city down. In each and every house there was just this one talk, one thought: 'There is no hope of safety for our race now; if his messenger was so unspeakably powerful, then what will be the outcome when the Master himself comes?" When Rāvan's principal queen Mandodarī heard from her emissaries regarding what the citizens were whispering she felt greatly disturbed. Meeting her lord alone she fell at his feet, and with joined palms besought him with words steeped in wisdom: "O my husband, cease to contend against Hari; take my words to your heart as a most wholesome advice. Whose mere messenger did such deeds that our matrons, on remembering him, miscarry, please send to him back his spouse with your personal minister—if you seek your welfare, my lord. Sītā has come here for the ruin of our entire race—alike a frosty night of destruction to the lilies of our family. Hearken, my lord: unless you give up Sītā, neither Shambhu nor Brahmmā can save you.

जब तें रामु ब्याहि घर आए । नित नव मंगल मोद बधाए ॥
दीन दयाल बिरिदु संभारी । हरहु नाथ मम संकट भारी ॥
मंगल भवन अमंगल हारी । द्रवउ सो दसरथ अजिर बिहारी ॥

दोहा-*dohā:*

राम बान अहि गन सरिस निकर निसाचर भेक ।
rāma bāna ahi gana sarisa nikara nisācara bheka,
जब लगि ग्रसत न तब लगि जतनु करहु तजि टेक ॥ ३६ ॥
jaba lagi grasata na taba lagi jatanu karahu taji ṭeka. 36 .

प्रबिसि नगर कीजे सब काजा । हृदयँ राखि कोसलपुर राजा ॥
जपहिं नामु जन आरत भारी । मिटहिं कुसंकट होहिं सुखारी ॥
सियावर राम जय जय राम । मेरे प्रभु राम जय जय राम ॥

Rāma's arrows are like serpents and the demon hosts are just so many frogs; give up your obstinacy and devise some means of safety before everything is lost."

Dt: ____________________

चौपाई-caupāī:

श्रवन सुनी सठ ता करि बानी । बिहसा जगत बिदित अभिमानी ॥
śravana sunī saṭha tā kari bānī, bihasā jagata bidita abhimānī .

सभय सुभाउ नारि कर साचा । मंगल महुँ भय मन अति काचा ॥
sabhaya subhāu nāri kara sācā, maṁgala mahuṁ bhaya mana ati kācā .

जौं आवइ मर्कट कटकाई । जिअहिं बिचारे निसिचर खाई ॥
jauṁ āvai markaṭa kaṭakāī, jiahiṁ bicāre nisicara khāī .

कंपहिं लोकप जाकीं त्रासा । तासु नारि सभीत बड़ि हासा ॥
kaṁpahiṁ lokapa jākīṁ trāsā, tāsu nāri sabhīta baṛi hāsā .

अस कहि बिहसि ताहि उर लाई । चलेउ सभाँ ममता अधिकाई ॥
asa kahi bihasi tāhi ura lāī, caleu sabhāṁ mamatā adhikāī .

मंदोदरी हृदयँ कर चिंता । भयउ कंत पर बिधि बिपरीता ॥
maṁdodarī hṛdayaṁ kara ciṁtā, bhayau kaṁta para bidhi biparītā .

बैठेउ सभाँ खबरि असि पाई । सिंधु पार सेना सब आई ॥
baiṭheu sabhāṁ khabari asi pāī, siṁdhu pāra senā saba āī .

बूझेसि सचिव उचित मत कहहू । ते सब हँसे मष्ट करि रहहू ॥
būjhesi saciva ucita mata kahahū, te saba haṁse maṣṭa kari rahahū .

जितेहु सुरासुर तब श्रम नाहीं । नर बानर केहि लेखे माहीं ॥
jitehu surāsura taba śrama nāhīṁ, nara bānara kehi lekhe māhīṁ .

When the foolish Rāvan—who was known the world over for his haughtiness—heard Mandodarī's admonitions, he guffawed, "A woman is naturally cast in a timorous mould and harbors fear even in propitious times. If the monkey troops come here, those poor wretches will be devoured by our demon hosts. The very guardians of spheres tremble in fear of me; how ridiculous that you, my wife, should display such fright." Saying so he laughed, and displaying much outward affection, embraced her. He then left for the council-chambers. Mandodarī however remained troubled at heart and sighed, 'Verily the heavens are against us.' As he occupied the royal seat in the chamber, Rāvan received intelligence that a whole army had become assembled on the other side of ocean. Thereupon he asked his councilors, "Advice to me the proper course." They all laughed and said, "What is to be said or done? With no trouble at all you have conquered all—be they god or demons—then of what consequence are these monkeys and men?"

दोहा-*dohā:*

सचिव बैद गुर तीनि जौं प्रिय बोलहिं भय आस ।
saciva baida gura tīni jaum̐ priya bolahim̐ bhaya āsa,
राज धर्म तन तीनि कर होइ बेगिहीं नास ॥३७॥
rāja dharma tana tīni kara hoi begihīm̐ nāsa. 37 .

When a minister, physician or Guru—these three—are using pleasing words out of fear or in hope of reward, then as a consequence, one's dominion, health and Dharma, all three, become quickly destroyed.

जब तें रामु ब्याहि घर आए । नित नव मंगल मोद बधाए ॥
दीन दयाल बिरिदु संभारी । हरहु नाथ मम संकट भारी ॥
मंगल भवन अमंगल हारी । द्रवउ सो दसरथ अजिर बिहारी ॥

प्रबिसि नगर कीजे सब काजा । हृदयँ राखि कोसलपुर राजा ॥
जपहिं नामु जन आरत भारी । मिटहिं कुसंकट होहिं सुखारी ॥
सियावर राम जय जय राम । मेरे प्रभु राम जय जय राम ॥

चौपाई-*caupāī:*

सोइ रावन कहुँ बनी सहाई । अस्तुति करहिं सुनाइ सुनाई ॥
soi rāvana kahum̐ banī sahāī, astuti karahiṁ sunāi sunāī .
अवसर जानि बिभीषनु आवा । भ्राता चरन सीसु तेहिं नावा ॥
avasara jāni bibhīṣanu āvā, bhrātā carana sīsu tehiṁ nāvā .
पुनि सिरु नाइ बैठ निज आसन । बोला बचन पाइ अनुसासन ॥
puni siru nāi baiṭha nija āsana, bolā bacana pāi anusāsana .
जौ कृपाल पूँछिहु मोहि बाता । मति अनुरुप कहउँ हित ताता ॥
jau kṛpāla pūm̐chihu mohi bātā, mati anurupa kahaum̐ hita tātā .
जो आपन चाहै कल्याना । सुजसु सुमति सुभ गति सुख नाना ॥
jo āpana cāhai kalyānā, sujasu sumati subha gati sukha nānā .
सो परनारि लिलार गोसाईं । तजउ चउथि के चंद कि नाईं ॥
so paranāri lilāra gosāīṁ, tajau cauthi ke caṁda ki nāīṁ .
चौदह भुवन एक पति होई । भूतद्रोह तिष्टइ नहिं सोई ॥
caudaha bhuvana eka pati hoī, bhūtadroha tiṣṭai nahiṁ soī .
गुन सागर नागर नर जोऊ । अलप लोभ भल कहइ न कोऊ ॥
guna sāgara nāgara nara joū, alapa lobha bhala kahai na koū .

Exactly the same thing was happening to Rāvan: his advisers did nothing but sound his praises. Perceiving it to be an opportune moment, Vibhishan came there and bowed his head at his brother's feet. Bowing again he took his seat and after obtaining permission said, "If you were to ask my opinion dear brother, I will tender it to the best of my ability and in your very best interest. Let him—who seeks his own welfare, good reputation, wisdom, a beneficial providence upon death, and every other happiness—avert his eyes from the face of another man's wife: just as one avoids the moon on the fourth night of lunar month. Even though a man be the sole lord of the fourteen spheres, he would certainly fall if he remains hostile towards others. No one speaks well of a greedy person who covets things of others—even if he were most clever and an ocean of virtues otherwise.

जब तें रामु ब्याहि घर आए । नित नव मंगल मोद बधाए ॥
दीन दयाल बिरिदु संभारी । हरहु नाथ मम संकट भारी ॥
मंगल भवन अमंगल हारी । द्रवउ सो दसरथ अजिर बिहारी ॥

दोहा-*dohā:*

काम क्रोध मद लोभ सब नाथ नरक के पंथ ।
kāma krodha mada lobha saba nātha naraka ke paṁtha,
सब परिहरि रघुबीरहि भजहु भजहिं जेहि संत ॥३८॥
saba parihari raghubīrahi bhajahu bhajahiṁ jehi saṁta. 38 .

Lust, wrath, vanity, and covetousness—are all the gateways to hell; abjure them and worship Raghubīr—He who is meditated upon by the saints.

Dt: ______________________________

प्रबिसि नगर कीजे सब काजा । हृदयँ राखि कोसलपुर राजा ॥
जपहिं नामु जन आरत भारी । मिटहिं कुसंकट होहिं सुखारी ॥
सियावर राम जय जय राम । मेरे प्रभु राम जय जय राम ॥

चौपाई-*caupāī:*

तात राम नहिं नर भूपाला । भुवनेस्वर कालहु कर काला ॥
tāta rāma nahiṁ nara bhūpālā, bhuvanesvara kālahu kara kālā .
ब्रह्म अनामय अज भगवंता । ब्यापक अजित अनादि अनंता ॥
brahma anāmaya aja bhagavaṁtā, byāpaka ajita anādi anaṁtā .
गो द्विज धेनु देव हितकारी । कृपा सिंधु मानुष तनुधारी ॥
go dvija dhenu deva hitakārī, kr̥pā siṁdhu mānuṣa tanudhārī .
जन रंजन भंजन खल ब्राता । बेद धर्म रच्छक सुनु भ्राता ॥
jana raṁjana bhaṁjana khala brātā, beda dharma racchaka sunu bhrātā .
ताहि बयरु तजि नाइअ माथा । प्रनतारति भंजन रघुनाथा ॥
tāhi bayaru taji nāia māthā, pranatārati bhaṁjana raghunāthā .
देहु नाथ प्रभु कहुँ बैदेही । भजहु राम बिनु हेतु सनेही ॥
dehu nātha prabhu kahum̐ baidehī, bhajahu rāma binu hetu sanehī .
सरन गएँ प्रभु ताहु न त्यागा । बिस्व द्रोह कृत अघ जेहि लागा ॥
sarana gaem̐ prabhu tāhu na tyāgā, bisva droha kr̥ta agha jehi lāgā .
जासु नाम त्रय ताप नसावन । सोइ प्रभु प्रगट समुझु जियँ रावन ॥
jāsu nāma traya tāpa nasāvana, soi prabhu pragaṭa samujhu jiyam̐ rāvana .

Rāma is no mere king but the King of kings—the invincible Ruler of the worlds, Death of Death himself. Rāma is Brahmn—the all-pervading Supreme Spirit, without a beginning and end, imperishable and uncreated, the unmanifest God. That very ocean of compassion has assumed a human form for the sake of good of the earth, the virtuous, pious, cows and the gods. Protector of the Vedas and Dharma, the savior of gods, Rāma has descended on earth to sport with his devotees and to break the ranks of the impious. O brother, give up all hostility to Rāma and bow your head to that Lord of Raghus—for He relieves the distress of every suppliant. O master, restore Videha's daughter to her Lord and worship Him—who is the impartial friend of all. The Lord never abandons one who surrenders to Him, even though he were guilty of causing ruin of the entire world. Know of this O Rāvan: the very same Lord God, whose very name is sufficient to destroy the threefold agonies, has manifested himself in human form as Shrī Rāma.

दोहा-*dohā:*

बार बार पद लागउँ बिनय करउँ दससीस ।
bāra bāra pada lāgaum̐ binaya karaum̐ dasasīsa,
परिहरि मान मोह मद भजहु कोसलाधीस ॥३९क ॥
parihari māna moha mada bhajahu kosalādhīsa. 39(ka) .

मुनि पुलस्ति निज सिष्य सन कहि पठई यह बात ।
muni pulasti nija siṣya sana kahi paṭhaī yaha bāta,
तुरत सो मैं प्रभु सन कही पाइ सुअवसरु तात ॥३९ख ॥
turata so maiṁ prabhu sana kahī pāi suavasaru tāta. 39(kha) .

Again and again I fall at your feet and make this supplication, O king: Abandon pride, infatuation and arrogance, and adore Shrī Rāma. Our grandsire Sage Pulastya just conveyed us a message with this proposition through his personal disciple—and availing myself of this opportunity, I have forthwith brought it to you brother."

जब तें रामु ब्याहि घर आए । नित नव मंगल मोद बधाए ॥
दीन दयाल बिरिदु संभारी । हरहु नाथ मम संकट भारी ॥
मंगल भवन अमंगल हारी । द्रवउ सो दसरथ अजिर बिहारी ॥

प्रबिसि नगर कीजे सब काजा । हृदयँ राखि कोसलपुर राजा ॥
जपहिं नामु जन आरत भारी । मिटहिं कुसंकट होहिं सुखारी ॥
सियावर राम जय जय राम । मेरे प्रभु राम जय जय राम ॥

Dt: ____________________

चौपाई-*caupāī:*

माल्यवंत अति सचिव सयाना । तासु बचन सुनि अति सुख माना ॥
mālyavaṁta ati saciva sayānā, tāsu bacana suni ati sukha mānā .
तात अनुज तव नीति बिभूषन । सो उर धरहु जो कहत बिभीषन ॥
tāta anuja tava nīti bibhūṣana, so ura dharahu jo kahata bibhīṣana .
रिपु उतकरष कहत सठ दोऊ । दूरि न करहु इहाँ हइ कोऊ ॥
ripu utakaraṣa kahata saṭha doū, dūri na karahu ihām̐ hai koū .
माल्यवंत गृह गयउ बहोरी । कहइ बिभीषनु पुनि कर जोरी ॥
mālyavaṁta gr̥ha gayau bahorī, kahai bibhīṣanu puni kara jorī .
सुमति कुमति सब कें उर रहहीं । नाथ पुरान निगम अस कहहीं ॥
sumati kumati saba kem̐ ura rahahīṁ, nātha purāna nigama asa kahahīṁ .
जहाँ सुमति तहँ संपति नाना । जहाँ कुमति तहँ बिपति निदाना ॥
jahām̐ sumati taham̐ sampati nānā, jahām̐ kumati taham̐ bipati nidānā .
तव उर कुमति बसी बिपरीता । हित अनहित मानहु रिपु प्रीता ॥
tava ura kumati basī biparītā, hita anahita mānahu ripu prītā .
कालराति निसिचर कुल केरी । तेहि सीता पर प्रीति घनेरी ॥
kālarāti nisicara kula kerī, tehi sītā para prīti ghanerī .

Malyavan, one of the wise counselors, greatly rejoiced hearing these words. "Your younger brother is the very ornament of wisdom; take to heart the admirable counsel of Vibhishan, my son." But Rāvan thundered, "Both these idiots dare glorify the enemy! Is there no one here who will remove them from my sight?" Malyavan thereupon returned to his home, but Vibhishan, with clasped hands, spoke yet again, "Wisdom and un-wisdom dwell in every heart, O master—so declare the Vedas and Purānas. Where there is wisdom, prosperity of every kind reigns; and where there is non-wisdom, misfortune is the inevitable result. Perversity has taken possession of your heart—that is why you consider your friends as foes and your foes as friends. And that is why you have become so extremely enamored of Sītā—who is the very Night of Death for the destruction of our race.

जब तें रामु ब्याहि घर आए । नित नव मंगल मोद बधाए ॥
दीन दयाल बिरिदु संभारी । हरहु नाथ मम संकट भारी ॥
मंगल भवन अमंगल हारी । द्रवउ सो दसरथ अजिर बिहारी ॥

दोहा-*dohā:*

तात चरन गहि मागउँ राखहु मोर दुलार ।
tāta carana gahi māgaum̐ rākhahu mora dulāra,
सीता देहु राम कहुँ अहित न होइ तुम्हार ॥४०॥
sītā dehu rāma kahum̐ ahita na hoi tumhāra. 40 .

प्रबिसि नगर कीजे सब काजा । हृदयँ राखि कोसलपुर राजा ॥
जपहिं नामु जन आरत भारी । मिटहिं कुसंकट होहिं सुखारी ॥
सियावर राम जय जय राम । मेरे प्रभु राम जय जय राम ॥

Clasping your feet, my brother, I beseech to you; please grant this prayer of mine as a token of our affection: restore Sītā to Rāma and absolutely nothing bad will happen to you I tell you."

Dt: ____________________

चौपाई-*caupāī:*

बुध पुरान श्रुति संमत बानी । कही बिभीषन नीति बखानी ॥
budha purāna śruti saṁmata bānī, kahī bibhīṣana nīti bakhānī .
सुनत दसानन उठा रिसाई । खल तोहि निकट मुत्यु अब आई ॥
sunata dasānana uṭhā risāī, khala tohi nikaṭa mutyu aba āī .
जिअसि सदा सठ मोर जिआवा । रिपु कर पच्छ मूढ़ तोहि भावा ॥
jiasi sadā saṭha mora jiāvā, ripu kara paccha mūṛha tohi bhāvā .
कहसि न खल अस को जग माहीं । भुज बल जाहि जिता मैं नाहीं ॥
kahasi na khala asa ko jaga māhīṁ, bhuja bala jāhi jitā maiṁ nāhīṁ .
मम पुर बसि तपसिन्ह पर प्रीती । सठ मिलु जाइ तिन्हहि कहु नीती ॥
mama pura basi tapasinha para prītī, saṭha milu jāi tinhahi kahu nītī .
अस कहि कीन्हेसि चरन प्रहारा । अनुज गहे पद बारहिं बारा ॥
asa kahi kīnhesi carana prahārā, anuja gahe pada bārahiṁ bārā .
उमा संत कइ इहइ बड़ाई । मंद करत जो करइ भलाई ॥
umā saṁta kai ihai baṛāī, maṁda karata jo karai bhalāī .
तुम्ह पितु सरिस भलेहिं मोहि मारा । रामु भजें हित नाथ तुम्हारा ॥
tumha pitu sarisa bhalehiṁ mohi mārā, rāmu bhajeṁ hita nātha tumhārā .
सचिव संग लै नभ पथ गयऊ । सबहि सुनाइ कहत अस भयऊ ॥
saciva saṁga lai nabha patha gayaū, sabahi sunāi kahata asa bhayaū .

The words which Vibhishan spoke were wise and prudent, supported by the authority of Vedas and Puranas, but the Ten-headed rose in great fury upon hearing them, "O wretch, your death is imminent now. You live on my generosity, fool—it is I who keeps you alive—and yet you favor the enemy's side! Tell me wretch, if there is any one in this world whom I have not conquered by the might of my arms! You dwell in my city and yet you cherish love for those hermits! Fool, better you go to them then and preach to them your wisdom." Saying so Rāvan kicked his brother away—but who still continued to clasp him by the feet pleading, "You are like a father to me—it is well that you have beaten me. But your welfare, my lord, lies in devotion to Shrī Rāma." O Umā, therein lies the greatness of a saint—who returns good even for evil. Eventually Vibhishan left taking his ministers along with him. As he made his way through the air, he announced loudly for all to hear:

जब तें रामु ब्याहि घर आए । नित नव मंगल मोद बधाए ॥
दीन दयाल बिरिदु संभारी । हरहु नाथ मम संकट भारी ॥
मंगल भवन अमंगल हारी । द्रवउ सो दसरथ अजिर बिहारी ॥

दोहा-*dohā:*

रामु सत्यसंकल्प प्रभु सभा कालबस तोरि ।
rāmu satyasaṁkalpa prabhu sabhā kālabasa tori,
मैं रघुबीर सरन अब जाउँ देहु जनि खोरि ॥४१॥
maiṁ raghubīra saraṇa aba jāuṁ dehu jani khori. 41 .

प्रबिसि नगर कीजे सब काजा । हृदयँ राखि कोसलपुर राजा ॥
जपहिं नामु जन आरत भारी । मिटहिं कुसंकट होहिं सुखारी ॥
सियावर राम जय जय राम । मेरे प्रभु राम जय जय राम ॥

“Rāma is the All-sufficient All-mighty Lord God who can destroy by His mere will. This council, overpowered by fate, seems destined to be doomed. I now seek refuge in Rāma, lay no blame upon me.”

Dt: ____________________

चौपाई-*caupāī:*

अस कहि चला बिभीषनु जबहीं । आयूहीन भए सब तबहीं ॥
asa kahi calā bibhīṣanu jabahīṁ, āyūhīna bhae saba tabahīṁ .
साधु अवग्या तुरत भवानी । कर कल्यान अखिल कै हानी ॥
sādhu avagyā turata bhavānī, kara kalyāna akhila kai hānī .
रावन जबहिं बिभीषन त्यागा । भयउ बिभव बिनु तबहिं अभागा ॥
rāvana jabahiṁ bibhīṣana tyāgā, bhayau bibhava binu tabahiṁ abhāgā .
चलेउ हरषि रघुनायक पाहीं । करत मनोरथ बहु मन माहीं ॥
caleu haraṣi raghunāyaka pāhīṁ, karata manoratha bahu mana māhīṁ .
देखिहउँ जाइ चरन जलजाता । अरुन मृदुल सेवक सुखदाता ॥
dekhihauṁ jāi carana jalajātā, aruna mṛdula sevaka sukhadātā .
जे पद परसि तरी रिषिनारी । दंडक कानन पावनकारी ॥
je pada parasi tarī riṣinārī, daṁḍaka kānana pāvanakārī .
जे पद जनकसुताँ उर लाए । कपट कुरंग संग धर धाए ॥
je pada janakasutāṁ ura lāe, kapaṭa kuraṁga saṁga dhara dhāe .
हर उर सर सरोज पद जेई । अहोभाग्य मैं देखिहउँ तेई ॥
hara ura sara saroja pada jeī, ahobhāgya maiṁ dekhihauṁ teī .

Speaking thusly Vibhishan left—and with his departure, their doom and death became sealed. Disrespect to a saint brings speedy ruin to one's propitiousness and prosperity. The moment he abandoned Vibhishan, that luckless wretch Rāvan lost all his glory and fortune. Joyfully Vibhishan proceeded to meet Shrī Rāma, his heart brimming with excitement and anticipation: "I am about to behold those lotus feet—so roseate, so delicate, so beneficent to all who wait upon them—those very feet which hallowed the paths of Daṁḍak forest and redeemed the Rishī's wife Ahalyā—the hallowed feet that Janak's daughter locked up in her heart, even while they moved to chase the delusive deer—and which feet dwell as pair of lotuses in the lake of Shiva's heart—how fortunate am I that I will get to see those very blessed feet.

दोहा-*dohā:*

जिन्ह पायन्ह के पादुकन्हि भरतु रहे मन लाइ ।
jinha pāyanha ke pādukanhi bharatu rahe mana lāī,
ते पद आजु बिलोकिहउँ इन्ह नयनन्हि अब जाइ ॥४२॥
te pada āju bilokihaum̐ inha nayananhi aba jāi. 42 .

Those very feet, even the wooden Pādukas of which are lovingly adored by Bharat, I shall this very day, and very soon, behold with my own eyes."

Dt: ____________________

चौपाई-*caupāī:*

एहिं बिधि करत सप्रेम बिचारा । आयउ सपदि सिंधु एहिं पारा ॥
ehi bidhi karata saprema bicārā, āyau sapadi siṁdhu ehiṁ pārā .
कपिन्ह बिभीषनु आवत देखा । जाना कोउ रिपु दूत बिसेषा ॥
kapinha bibhīṣanu āvata dekhā, jānā kou ripu dūta biseṣā .
ताहि राखि कपीस पहिं आए । समाचार सब ताहि सुनाए ॥
tāhi rākhi kapīsa pahiṁ āe, samācāra saba tāhi sunāe .
कह सुग्रीव सुनहु रघुराई । आवा मिलन दसानन भाई ॥
kaha sugrīva sunahu raghurāī, āvā milana dasānana bhāī .
कह प्रभु सखा बूझिऐ काहा । कहइ कपीस सुनहु नरनाहा ॥
kaha prabhu sakhā būjhiai kāhā, kahai kapīsa sunahu naranāhā .
जानि न जाइ निसाचर माया । कामरूप केहि कारन आया ॥
jāni na jāi nisācara māyā, kāmarūpa kehi kārana āyā .
भेद हमार लेन सठ आवा । राखिअ बाँधि मोहि अस भावा ॥
bheda hamāra lena saṭha āvā, rākhia bāṁdhi mohi asa bhāvā .
सखा नीति तुम्ह नीकि बिचारी । मम पन सरनागत भयहारी ॥
sakhā nīti tumha nīki bicārī, mama pana saranāgata bhayahārī .
सुनि प्रभु बचन हरष हनुमाना । सरनागत बच्छल भगवाना ॥
suni prabhu bacana haraṣa hanumānā, saranāgata bacchala bhagavānā .

With such loving fancies to occupy his mind, Vibhishan quickly arrived on this side of the ocean. Seeing him arrive, the monkeys took him to be some special envoy of the enemy; so therefore they detained him outside and went calling to their chiefs with the news. Said Sugrīv, "Hearken O Raghurai, Rāvan's brother has come to meet you." And the Lord asked, "What do you advice friend?" The monkey-king replied, "Mark my words Sire, the craftiness of demons is past all telling, their nefarious ways can not be fathomed. Though capable of assuming any form, wherefore he comes here in person—that's a mystery. Perhaps the fool has come here to spy out our secrets; I would fain detain him and keep him a prisoner." Whereupon Rāma said, "Friend, you have reasoned well and with much worldly wisdom; but my vow is to dispel the fears of all those who seek refuge in me." Hanumān rejoiced to hear these words of the Lord—who cherishes affection for a suppliant even as a parent does.

जब तें रामु ब्याहि घर आए । नित नव मंगल मोद बधाए ॥
दीन दयाल बिरिदु संभारी । हरहु नाथ मम संकट भारी ॥
मंगल भवन अमंगल हारी । द्रवउ सो दसरथ अजिर बिहारी ॥

दोहा-*dohā:*

सरनागत कहुँ जे तजहिं निज अनहित अनुमानि ।
saranāgata kahum̐ je tajahiṁ nija anahita anumāni,
ते नर पावँर पापमय तिन्हहि बिलोकत हानि ॥४३॥
te nara pāvam̐ra pāpamaya tinhahi bilokata hāni. 43 .

प्रबिसि नगर कीजे सब काजा । हृदयँ राखि कोसलपुर राजा ॥
जपहिं नामु जन आरत भारी । मिटहिं कुसंकट होहिं सुखारी ॥
सियावर राम जय जय राम । मेरे प्रभु राम जय जय राम ॥

"Such people are vile and sinful, and their very sight is abominable who—apprehending ill for themselves—forsake someone who has come genuinely in full surrender, seeking shelter.

Dt: ______________________

चौपाई-*caupāī:*

कोटि बिप्र बध लागहिं जाहू । आएँ सरन तजउँ नहिं ताहू ॥
koṭi bipra badha lāgahiṁ jāhū, āeṁ sarana tajauṁ nahiṁ tāhū .
सनमुख होइ जीव मोहि जबहीं । जन्म कोटि अघ नासहिं तबहीं ॥
sanamukha hoi jīva mohi jabahīṁ, janma koṭi agha nāsahiṁ tabahīṁ .
पापवंत कर सहज सुभाऊ । भजनु मोर तेहि भाव न काऊ ॥
pāpavaṁta kara sahaja subhāū, bhajanu mora tehi bhāva na kāū .
जौं पै दुष्टहदय सोइ होई । मोरें सनमुख आव कि सोई ॥
jauṁ pai duṣṭahadaya soi hoī, moreṁ sanamukha āva ki soī .
निर्मल मन जन सो मोहि पावा । मोहि कपट छल छिद्र न भावा ॥
nirmala mana jana so mohi pāvā, mohi kapaṭa chala chidra na bhāvā .
भेद लेन पठवा दससीसा । तबहुँ न कछु भय हानि कपीसा ॥
bheda lena paṭhavā dasasīsā, tabahuṁ na kachu bhaya hāni kapīsā .
जग महुँ सखा निसाचर जेते । लछिमनु हनइ निमिष महुँ तेते ॥
jaga mahuṁ sakhā nisācara jete, lachimanu hanai nimiṣa mahuṁ tete .
जौं सभीत आवा सरनाई । रखिहउँ ताहि प्रान की नाईं ॥
jauṁ sabhīta āvā saranāīṁ, rakhihauṁ tāhi prāna kī nāīṁ .

I will not abandon even the slayer of a myriad Brahmins, were he to seek refuge in me. The moment they turn their face to me, the sins accrued through millions of lives of the Jivas get washed out. By their very nature, someone who is sinful can never take delight in my worship. Had Vibhishan been wicked at heart, could he have dared make it in my presence? Such alone—who have a pure heart—can attain to me. I have aversion for duplicity, hypocrisy, wile and deceit. And even if Rāvan has sent him here to spy out our secrets, then too we have nothing to fear or lose O monkey-chief. My friend, Lakshman can dispose of in a trice all the demons that this world may hold; and if he has come here out of fear, seeking my protection, then I will protect him as I would my own life.

जब तें रामु ब्याहि घर आए । नित नव मंगल मोद बधाए ॥
दीन दयाल बिरिदु संभारी । हरहु नाथ मम संकट भारी ॥
मंगल भवन अमंगल हारी । द्रवउ सो दसरथ अजिर बिहारी ॥

दोहा-*dohā:*

उभय भाँति तेहि आनहु हँसि कह कृपानिकेत ।
ubhaya bhām̐ti tehi ānahu ham̐si kaha kṛpāniketa,
जय कृपाल कहि कपि चले अंगद हनू समेत ॥ ४४ ॥
jaya kṛpāla kahi kapi cale aṁgada hanū sameta. 44 .

प्रबिसि नगर कीजे सब काजा । हृदयँ राखि कोसलपुर राजा ॥
जपहिं नामु जन आरत भारी । मिटहिं कुसंकट होहिं सुखारी ॥
सियावर राम जय जय राम । मेरे प्रभु राम जय जय राम ॥

In either case have him brought here," thus spake the All-Merciful with a smile. "Glory be Thine, O merciful Lord," shouted the monkeys as they went with Aṁgad and Hanumān to usher in Vibhishan.

चौपाई-*caupāī:*

सादर तेहि आगें करि बानर । चले जहाँ रघुपति करुनाकर ॥
sādara tehi āgeṁ kari bānara, cale jahām̐ raghupati karunākara .
दूरिहि ते देखे द्वौ भ्राता । नयनानंद दान के दाता ॥
dūrihi te dekhe dvau bhrātā, nayanānaṁda dāna ke dātā .
बहुरि राम छबिधाम बिलोकी । रहेउ ठटुकि एकटक पल रोकी ॥
bahuri rāma chabidhāma bilokī, raheu ṭhaṭuki ekaṭaka pala rokī .
भुज प्रलंब कंजारुन लोचन । स्यामल गात प्रनत भय मोचन ॥
bhuja pralaṁba kaṁjāruna locana, syāmala gāta pranata bhaya mocana .
सिंघ कंध आयत उर सोहा । आनन अमित मदन मन मोहा ॥
siṁgha kaṁdha āyata ura sohā, ānana amita madana mana mohā .
नयन नीर पुलकित अति गाता । मन धरि धीर कही मृदु बाता ॥
nayana nīra pulakita ati gātā, mana dhari dhīra kahī mṛdu bātā .
नाथ दसानन कर मैं भ्राता । निसिचर बंस जनम सुरत्राता ॥
nātha dasānana kara maiṁ bhrātā, nisicara baṁsa janama suratrātā .
सहज पापप्रिय तामस देहा । जथा उलूकहि तम पर नेहा ॥
sahaja pāpapriya tāmasa dehā, jathā ulūkahi tama para nehā .

Placing Vibhishan ahead, they respectfully escorted him into the presence of Raghupati, the mine of compassion. Vibhishan beheld from a distance the two brothers—the duo who impart unending bliss by their very blessed sight. Looking upon Rāma's perfect beauty, he stood stock-still, his gaze intently fixed. Vibhishan beheld the beautiful form of Rāma—the long arms, the red lotus-like eyes, swarthy limbs which rid the suppliant of all fears, the dark-hued body with lion-like shoulders, magnificent wide chest and a most charming face—beauty which would ravish the soul of Kāmadev himself. With eyes tearing up and trembling limbs, Vibhishan at last composed himself enough to speak in accents most mild: "My Lord, I am Rāvan's brother. I am born of the demon race of savage temperament and I am as naturally prone to evil as an owl is partial to the dark night, O Protector of gods.

दोहा-dohā:

श्रवन सुजसु सुनि आयउँ प्रभु भंजन भव भीर ।
śravana sujasu suni āyaum̐ prabhu bhamjana bhava bhīra,
त्राहि त्राहि आरति हरन सरन सुखद रघुबीर ॥४५॥
trāhi trāhi ārati harana sarana sukhada raghubīra. 45 .

Having heard with my ears of Thy fair renown I have come to Thee—knowing my Lord to be the dissipater of all the fears of existence. Save me, O save me Raghubīr, O reliever of distress, O giver of joys, I have come seeking refuge in Thee."

चौपाई-*caupāī:*

अस कहि करत दंडवत देखा । तुरत उठे प्रभु हरष बिसेषा ॥
asa kahi karata daṁḍavata dekhā, turata uṭhe prabhu haraṣa biseṣā .
दीन बचन सुनि प्रभु मन भावा । भुज बिसाल गहि हृदयँ लगावा ॥
dīna bacana suni prabhu mana bhāvā, bhuja bisāla gahi hṛdayaṁ lagāvā.
अनुज सहित मिलि ढिग बैठारी । बोले बचन भगत भयहारी ॥
anuja sahita mili ḍhiga baiṭhārī, bole bacana bhagata bhayahārī .
कहु लंकेस सहित परिवारा । कुसल कुठाहर बास तुम्हारा ॥
kahu laṁkesa sahita parivārā, kusala kuṭhāhara bāsa tumhārā .
खल मंडलीं बसहु दिनु राती । सखा धरम निबहइ केहि भाँती ॥
khala maṁḍalīṁ basahu dinu rātī, sakhā dharama nibahai kehi bhāṁtī .
मैं जानउँ तुम्हारि सब रीती । अति नय निपुन न भाव अनीती ॥
maiṁ jānauṁ tumhāri saba rītī, ati naya nipuna na bhāva anītī .
बरु भल बास नरक कर ताता । दुष्ट संग जनि देइ बिधाता ॥
baru bhala bāsa naraka kara tātā, duṣṭa saṁga jani dei bidhātā .
अब पद देखि कुसल रघुराया । जौं तुम्ह कीन्हि जानि जन दाया ॥
aba pada dekhi kusala raghurāyā, jauṁ tumha kīnhi jāni jana dāyā .

When he saw Vibhishan falling prostrate uttering these words, the Lord arose hastily and full of joy. The humble speech of Vibhishan charmed the Lord, and he, of long arms, clasped the suppliant to his heart. Having, along with his brother, thus welcomed Vibhishan, the Lord seated him by his side and spoke words to allay his votary of every fear, "Tell me, O king of Lankā, is all well with you and your family? You dwell in a deplorable place; day and night you live in the midst of wicked multitudes—how then are you able to maintain your piety, my friend? I know all your circumstance: your propensity for virtue and aversion to evil. My friend, it is better to live in hell rather than in the company of evil." "All is well with me now that I behold your lotus feet, Raghurai. Blessed am I that you shower me with your mercy—recognizing me to be your servant."

जब तें रामु ब्याहि घर आए । नित नव मंगल मोद बधाए ॥
दीन दयाल बिरिदु संभारी । हरहु नाथ मम संकट भारी ॥
मंगल भवन अमंगल हारी । द्रवउ सो दसरथ अजिर बिहारी ॥

दोहा-*dohā:*

तब लगि कुसल न जीव कहुँ सपनेहुँ मन बिश्राम ।
taba lagi kusala na jīva kahum̐ sapanehum̐ mana biśrāma;
जब लगि भजत न राम कहुँ सोक धाम तजि काम ॥४६॥
jaba lagi bhajata na rāma kahum̐ soka dhāma taji kāma. 46 .

प्रबिसि नगर कीजे सब काजा । हृदयँ राखि कोसलपुर राजा ॥
जपहिं नामु जन आरत भारी । मिटहिं कुसंकट होहिं सुखारी ॥
सियावर राम जय जय राम । मेरे प्रभु राम जय जय राम ॥

[Said Shiva:] No Jiva can have any worldly wellbeing nor have any semblance of peace—even in dream—until he worships Rāma having forsworn lust—that perennial fount of sorrows and remorse.

Dt: ____________________

चौपाई-*caupāī:*

तब लगि हृदयँ बसत खल नाना । लोभ मोह मच्छर मद माना ॥
tāba lagi hṛdayam̐ basata khala nānā, lobha moha macchara madā mānā .
जब लगि उर न बसत रघुनाथा । धरें चाप सायक कटि भाथा ॥
jaba lagi ura na basata raghunāthā, dhareṁ cāpa sāyaka kaṭi bhāthā .
ममता तरुन तमी अँधिआरी । राग द्वेष उलूक सुखकारी ॥
mamatā taruna tamī am̐dhiārī, rāga dveṣa ulūka sukhakārī .
तब लगि बसति जीव मन माहीं । जब लगि प्रभु प्रताप रबि नाहीं ॥
taba lagi basati jīva mana māhīṁ, jaba lagi prabhu pratāpa rabi nāhīṁ .
अब मैं कुसल मिटे भय भारे । देखि राम पद कमल तुम्हारे ॥
aba maiṁ kusala miṭe bhaya bhāre, dekhi rāma pada kamala tumhāre .
तुम्ह कृपाल जा पर अनुकूला । ताहि न ब्याप त्रिबिध भव सूला ॥
tumha kṛpāla jā para anukūlā, tāhi na byāpa tribidha bhava sūlā .
मैं निसिचर अति अधम सुभाऊ । सुभ आचरनु कीन्ह नहिं काऊ ॥
maiṁ nisicara ati adhama subhāū, subha ācaranu kīnha nahiṁ kāū .
जासु रूप मुनि ध्यान न आवा । तेहिं प्रभु हरषि हृदयँ मोहि लावा ॥
jāsu rūpa muni dhyāna na āvā, tehiṁ prabhu haraṣi hṛdayam̐ mohi lāvā .

The villainous crew—greed, infatuation, jealousy, arrogance, pride—haunts the mind only so long as Raghunāth—armed with bow, arrows and a quiver fastened to his waist—does not take up his abode there. The intensely darkly night of worldly attachments—so agreeable to the owl-like passions of infatuation and hate—abides in the soul only so long as the Sun of the Lord's glory does not glow there. "Now that I have beheld your lotus feet, O Rāma, I am completely well and my gravest fears have been put to rest. The Threefold torments of Existence cease to have any effect upon those to whom you, in your mercy, show favor. I am a demon, of utterly vile nature, who never performed any goodly acts; and yet my Lord—whose divine vision even the saints scarcely attain despite their many profound meditations—has been pleased to take me to his heart.

जब तें रामु ब्याहि घर आए । नित नव मंगल मोद बधाए ॥
दीन दयाल बिरिदु संभारी । हरहु नाथ मम संकट भारी ॥
मंगल भवन अमंगल हारी । द्रवउ सो दसरथ अजिर बिहारी ॥

दोहा-*dohā:*

अहोभाग्य मम अमित अति राम कृपा सुख पुंज ।
ahobhāgya mama amita ati rāma kṛpā sukha pum̐ja,
देखेउँ नयन बिरंचि सिव सेब्य जुगल पद कंज ॥४७॥
dekheum̐ nayana biram̐ci siva sebya jugala pada kam̐ja. 47 .

प्रबिसि नगर कीजे सब काजा । हृदयँ राखि कोसलपुर राजा ॥
जपहिं नामु जन आरत भारी । मिटहिं कुसंकट होहिं सुखारी ॥
सियावर राम जय जय राम । मेरे प्रभु राम जय जय राम ॥

O All-gracious, All-blissful Rāma, I am blessed beyond measure in that I behold with my own eyes these hallowed lotus-feet—which even gods like Brahmmā and Shiva so lovingly adore."

Dt: ______________________

चौपाई-*caupāī:*

सुनहु सखा निज कहउँ सुभाऊ । जान भुसुंडि संभु गिरिजाऊ ॥
sunahu sakhā nija kahaum̐ subhāū, jāna bhusum̐ḍi sam̐bhu girijāū .
जौं नर होइ चराचर द्रोही । आवे सभय सरन तकि मोही ॥
jaum̐ nara hoi carācara drohī, āve sabhaya sarana taki mohī .
तजि मद मोह कपट छल नाना । करउँ सद्य तेहि साधु समाना ॥
taji mada moha kapaṭa chala nānā, karaum̐ sadya tehi sādhu samānā .
जननी जनक बंधु सुत दारा । तनु धनु भवन सुहृद परिवारा ॥
jananī janaka bam̐dhu suta dārā, tanu dhanu bhavana suhrada parivārā .
सब कै ममता ताग बटोरी । मम पद मनहि बाँध बरि डोरी ॥
saba kai mamatā tāga baṭorī, mama pada manahi bām̐dha bari ḍorī .
समदरसी इच्छा कछु नाहीं । हरष सोक भय नहिं मन माहीं ॥
samadarasī icchā kachu nāhīm̐, haraṣa soka bhaya nahim̐ mana māhīm̐ .
अस सज्जन मम उर बस कैसें । लोभी हृदयँ बसइ धनु जैसें ॥
asa sajjana mama ura basa kaisem̐, lobhī hṛdayam̐ basai dhanu jaisem̐ .
तुम्ह सारिखे संत प्रिय मोरें । धरउँ देह नहिं आन निहोरें ॥
tumha sārikhe sam̐ta priya morem̐, dharaum̐ deha nahim̐ āna nihorem̐ .

"Listen friend; let me tell you something of my nature—which is well known to Bhushundi, Shambhu, Girijā and others: If a person—even one who has been the curse of the whole world—comes in fear and complete surrender to me, abjuring all his pride and sensuality, without any subterfuge or guile, then I cast him at once into the very likeliness of a saint. The ties of affection which bind a person to mother, father, sibling, son, spouse, and to body, wealth, house, friends, relatives—are like so many strings; and those very strings, a wise and pious soul gathers up and twists into a cord—wherewith he binds himself unto my feet. With a mind freed of joy, grief and fear, such a one looks upon all beings with an eye of equanimity—devoid of all cravings. A saint of such description abides in my heart even as mammon resides in the heart of a covetous man. Saintly people like you are very dear to me, and it is only for their sake, and for no other reason, that I become Incarnate from Age to Age.

दोहा-*dohā:*

सगुन उपासक परहित निरत नीति दृढ़ नेम ।
saguna upāsaka parahita nirata nīti dṛṛha nema,
ते नर प्रान समान मम जिन्ह कें द्विज पद प्रेम ॥४८॥
ṭe naṛa prāna samāna mama jinha keṁ dvija pada pṛemạ. 48 .

Those who worship the Personal form of the Impersonal Unmanifest God, who are steadfast in uprightness, strict in pious observances, and who love and revere the twice-born—such people are dear to me like life itself.

चौपाई-*caupāī:*

सुनु लंकेस सकल गुन तोरें । तातें तुम्ह अतिसय प्रिय मोरें ॥
sunu laṁkesa sakala guna toreṁ, tāteṁ tumha atisaya priya moreṁ .
राम बचन सुनि बानर जूथा । सकल कहहिं जय कृपा बरूथा ॥
rāma bacana suni bānara jūthā, sakala kahahiṁ jaya kṛpā barūthā .
सुनत बिभीषनु प्रभु कै बानी । नहिं अघात श्रवनामृत जानी ॥
sunata bibhīṣanu prabhu kai bānī, nahiṁ aghāta śravanāmṛta jānī .
पद अंबुज गहि बारहिं बारा । हृदयँ समात न प्रेमु अपारा ॥
pada aṁbuja gahi bārahiṁ bārā, hṛdayaṁ samāta na premu apārā .
सुनहु देव सचराचर स्वामी । प्रनतपाल उर अंतरजामी ॥
sunahu deva sacarācara svāmī, pranatapāla ura aṁtarajāmī .
उर कछु प्रथम बासना रही । प्रभु पद प्रीति सरित सो बही ॥
ura kachu prathama bāsanā rahī, prabhu pada prīti sarita so bahī .
अब कृपाल निज भगति पावनी । देहु सदा सिव मन भावनी ॥
aba kṛpāla nija bhagati pāvanī, dehu sadā siva mana bhāvanī .
एवमस्तु कहि प्रभु रनधीरा । मागा तुरत सिंधु कर नीरा ॥
evamastu kahi prabhu ranadhīrā, māgā turata siṁdhu kara nīrā .
जदपि सखा तव इच्छा नाहीं । मोर दरसु अमोघ जग माहीं ॥
jadapi sakhā tava icchā nāhīṁ, mora darasu amogha jaga māhīṁ .
अस कहि राम तिलक तेहि सारा । सुमन बृष्टि नभ भई अपारा ॥
asa kahi rāma tilaka tehi sārā, sumana bṛṣṭi nabha bhaī apārā .

Listen O king of Lankā, you possess all these virtues and hence are very dear to me." On hearing these words of Shrī Rāma all the assembled monkeys cried out, "Glory to the All-merciful Lord!" The words of the Lord-God were like ambrosia to Vibhishan's ear, and unable to contain himself, and with his heart overflowing with joy, he clasped the Lord's feet again and again, saying "Hear O God, O Lord of all creation, O protector of the suppliant, O knower of all hearts: Hitherto, perchance I had some lurking desires in my heart, but forthwith they have all been washed away in the ebullient stream of devotion that now flows in my heart. Now, O gracious Lord, please grant me that very pure devotion to your holy feet which ever gladdens the heart of Lord Shiva." "Let that be so", averred the All-mighty valiant Lord; and then he asked for some water of the ocean to be brought there. "Even though you have no cravings, my friend, but in this world, the beholding of my sight invariably brings a reward all its own." Saying so, Rāma performed the *Rāj-Tilak* on his forehead—thereby bestowing the sovereignty of Lankā upon Vibhishan. An infinite shower of flowers rained down from the heavens.

जब तें रामु ब्याहि घर आए । नित नव मंगल मोद बधाए ॥
दीन दयाल बिरिदु संभारी । हरहु नाथ मम संकट भारी ॥
मंगल भवन अमंगल हारी । द्रवउ सो दसरथ अजिर बिहारी ॥

दोहा-*dohā:*

रावन क्रोध अनल निज स्वास समीर प्रचंड ।
rāvana krodha anala nija svāsa samīra pracaṁḍa,
जरत बिभीषनु राखेउ दीन्हेउ राजु अखंड ॥४९क॥
jarata bibhīṣanu rākheu dīnheu rāju akhaṁḍa. 49(ka) .

जो संपति सिव रावनहि दीन्हि दिएँ दस माथ ।
jo saṁpati siva rāvanahi dīnhi dieṁ dasa mātha,
सोइ संपदा बिभीषनहि सकुचि दीन्ह रघुनाथ ॥४९ख॥
soi saṁpadā bibhīṣanahi sakuci dīnha raghunātha. 49(kha) .

प्रबिसि नगर कीजे सब काजा । हृदयँ राखि कोसलपुर राजा ॥
जपहिं नामु जन आरत भारी । मिटहिं कुसंकट होहिं सुखारी ॥
सियावर राम जय जय राम । मेरे प्रभु राम जय जय राम ॥

Thus did Raghunāth protect Vibhishan—who was burning having being been consumed by the fiery wrath of Rāvan which had been fanned to fury by Vibhishan's own exhalation of words. Nay, the Lord Raghunāth—with no ostentation and with much humility—conferred upon Vibhishan that very fortune which Lord Shiva had given to Rāvan when he had offered his ten heads in sacrifice.

Dt: ____________________

चौपाई-*caupāī:*

अस प्रभु छाड़ि भजहिं जे आना । ते नर पसु बिनु पूँछ बिषाना ॥
asa prabhu chāṛi bhajahiṁ je ānā, te nara pasu binu pūm̐cha biṣānā .
निज जन जानि ताहि अपनावा । प्रभु सुभाव कपि कुल मन भावा ॥
nija jana jāni tāhi apanāvā, prabhu subhāva kapi kula mana bhāvā .
पुनि सर्बग्य सर्ब उर बासी । सर्बरूप सब रहित उदासी ॥
puni sarbagya sarba ura bāsī, sarbarūpa saba rahita udāsī .
बोले बचन नीति प्रतिपालक । कारन मनुज दनुज कुल घालक ॥
bole bacana nīti pratipālaka, kārana manuja danuja kula ghālaka .
सुनु कपीस लंकापति बीरा । केहि बिधि तरिअ जलधि गंभीरा ॥
sunu kapīsa laṁkāpati bīrā, kehi bidhi taria jaladhi gaṁbhīrā .
संकुल मकर उरग झष जाती । अति अगाध दुस्तर सब भाँती ॥
saṁkula makara uraga jhaṣa jātī, ati agādha dustara saba bhām̐tī .
कह लंकेस सुनहु रघुनायक । कोटि सिंधु सोषक तव सायक ॥
kaha laṁkesa sunahu raghunāyaka, koṭi siṁdhu soṣaka tava sāyaka .
जद्यपि तदपि नीति असि गाई । बिनय करिअ सागर सन जाई ॥
jadyapi tadapi nīti asi gāī, binaya karia sāgara sana jāī .

Those who forsake such a God, or worship another, are mere animals without tails or horns. Recognizing Vibhishan as his own, the Lord accepted him in his service. The good nature of their amiable Lord gladdened the hearts of all monkeys. Then the All-wise who dewlleth in all hearts, who is the formless reality that has become manifest as all these forms, who moves all this creation yet remains unmoved and unattached, who is the Formless-Absolute who became Incarnate to exterminate the wicked—spoke the following words, strictly to observe the rules of decorum: "Hearken O monkey-king and O valiant monarch of Lankā: how are we to cross this deep ocean, teeming with alligators, serpents, sea-monsters and other things, which is of fathomless depths and so difficult to cross whichever way one looks?" Vibhishan replied, "Hearken, O Raghunāyak: your arrows can burn down a thousand seas, but propriety dictates that we approach the ocean first and make petitions to that god to allow us a passage through.

जब तें रामु ब्याहि घर आए । नित नव मंगल मोद बधाए ॥
दीन दयाल बिरिदु संभारी । हरहु नाथ मम संकट भारी ॥
मंगल भवन अमंगल हारी । द्रवउ सो दसरथ अजिर बिहारी ॥

दोहा-dohā:

प्रभु तुम्हार कुलगुर जलधि कहिहि उपाय बिचारि ।
prabhu tumhāra kulagura jaladhi kahihi upāya bicāri,
बिनु प्रयास सागर तरिहि सकल भालु कपि धारि ॥५०॥
binu prayāsa sāgara tarihi sakala bhālu kapi dhāri. 50 .

प्रबिसि नगर कीजे सब काजा । हृदयँ राखि कोसलपुर राजा ॥
जपहिं नामु जन आरत भारी । मिटहिं कुसंकट होहिं सुखारी ॥
सियावर राम जय जय राम । मेरे प्रभु राम जय जय राम ॥

My lord, the deity presiding over the ocean is an ancestor in your lineage. Surely he can suggest some means whereby this army of bears and monkeys can get across the sea without trouble."

Dt: ______________

चौपाई-*caupāī:*

सखा कही तुम्ह नीकि उपाई । करिअ दैव जौं होइ सहाई ॥
sakhā kahī tumha nīki upāī, karia daiva jauṁ hoi sahāī .
मंत्र न यह लछिमन मन भावा । राम बचन सुनि अति दुख पावा ॥
maṁtra na yaha lachimana mana bhāvā, rāma bacana suni ati dukha pāvā .
नाथ दैव कर कवन भरोसा । सोषिअ सिंधु करिअ मन रोसा ॥
nātha daiva kara kavana bharosā, soṣia siṁdhu karia mana rosā .
कादर मन कहुँ एक अधारा । दैव दैव आलसी पुकारा ॥
kādara mana kahuṁ eka adhārā, daiva daiva ālasī pukārā .
सुनत बिहसि बोले रघुबीरा । ऐसेहिं करब धरहु मन धीरा ॥
sunata bihasi bole raghubīrā, aisehiṁ karaba dharahu mana dhīrā .
अस कहि प्रभु अनुजहि समुझाई । सिंधु समीप गए रघुराई ॥
asa kahi prabhu anujahi samujhāī, siṁdhu samīpa gae raghurāī .
प्रथम प्रनाम कीन्ह सिरु नाई । बैठे पुनि तट दर्भ डसाई ॥
prathama pranāma kīnha siru nāī, baiṭhe puni taṭa darbha ḍasāī .
जबहिं बिभीषन प्रभु पहिं आए । पाछें रावन दूत पठाए ॥
jabahiṁ bibhīṣana prabhu pahiṁ āe, pācheṁ rāvana dūta paṭhāe .

"You speak wisely my friend; let's do so and see if providence is of any help." But Lakshman did not like this counsel and was pained at the prospect of delay. He yearned to strike immediately. "Only the timorous hold onto the crutches of heavens and providences. It is only the sluggards that are found crying 'god, god'. Why trust in fate and god, my Lord? With your wrath, dry up this ocean at once." Raghubīr laughed and said, "Yes, that's what we shall do, but for now pray ease your mind and wait." In this way reassuring his brother Raghurai proceeded towards the seashore; and after bowing to the ocean, sat down on a spread of Kusha-grass. Meanwhile, after Vibhishan left to join Shri Rāma, Rāvan sent out some spies to follow him.

दोहा-doha:

सकल चरित तिन्ह देखे धरें कपट कपि देह ।

sakala carita tinha dekhe dhareṁ kapaṭa kapi deha,

प्रभु गुन हृदयँ सराहहिं सरनागत पर नेह ॥५१॥

prabhu guna hṛdayam̐ sarāhahiṁ saranāgata para neha. 51 .

The spies—disguised as monkeys—saw all that was happening there. Seeing the generosity of the Lord and his tender disposition, their hearts became filled with profound admiration.

Dt: ____________________

चौपाई-*caupāī:*

प्रगट बखानहिं राम सुभाऊ । अति सप्रेम गा बिसरि दुराऊ ॥
pragaṭa bakhānahiṁ rāma subhāū, ati saprema gā bisari durāū .
रिपु के दूत कपिन्ह तब जाने । सकल बाँधि कपीस पहिं आने ॥
ripu ke dūta kapinha taba jāne, sakala bām̐dhi kapīsa pahiṁ āne .
कह सुग्रीव सुनहु सब बानर । अंग भंग करि पठवहु निसिचर ॥
kaha sugrīva sunahu saba bānara, aṁga bhaṁga kari paṭhavahu nisicara
सुनि सुग्रीव बचन कपि धाए । बाँधि कटक चहु पास फिराए ॥
suni sugrīva bacana kapi dhāe, bām̐dhi kaṭaka cahu pāsa phirāe .
बहु प्रकार मारन कपि लागे । दीन पुकारत तदपि न त्यागे ॥
bahu prakāra mārana kapi lāge, dīna pukārata tadapi na tyāge .
जो हमार हर नासा काना । तेहि कोसलाधीस कै आना ॥
jo hamāra hara nāsā kānā, tehi kosalādhīsa kai ānā .
सुनि लछिमन सब निकट बोलाए । दया लागि हँसि तुरत छोड़ाए ॥
suni lachimana saba nikaṭa bolāe, dayā lāgi ham̐si turata choṛāe .
रावन कर दीजहु यह पाती । लछिमन बचन बाचु कुलघाती ॥
rāvana kara dījahu yaha pātī, lachimana bacana bācu kulaghātī .

In the intensity of their devotion; the spies forgot their guise and began extolling the Lord's magnanimity—and their camouflage dropped. Recognizing those to be the enemy spies, the monkeys caught them and took them to Sugrīv who ordained, "Mutilate them, then turn them back." Bound and gagged, the demons were paraded throughout the camp, with the monkeys beating them variously and refusing to let them go for all their pleas for mercy—until at last they cried, "We adjure you in the name of Rāma, please do not to rob us of our ears and nose." When Lakshman heard the commotion, he had them brought before him. Moved with compassion he smiled and had the demon-spies set free. Then giving them a letter he said, "Give this to Rāvan, and tell the destroyer of his race to read what Lakshman has to say.

दोहा-dohā:

कहेहु मुखागर मूढ़ सन मम संदेसु उदार ।

kahehu mukhāgara mūṛha sana mama saṁdesu udāra,

सीता देइ मिलेहु न त आवा कालु तुम्हार ॥५२॥

sītā dei milehu na ta āvā kālu tumhāra. 52 .

Further convey to that fool by words of mouth my magnanimous message: Surrender Sītā and make peace, or your final hour is near."

Dt: ____________________

चौपाई-*caupāī:*

तुरत नाइ लछिमन पद माथा । चले दूत बरनत गुन गाथा ॥
turata nāi lachimana pada māthā, cale dūta baranata guna gāthā .
कहत राम जसु लंकाँ आए । रावन चरन सीस तिन्ह नाए ॥
kahata rāma jasu laṁkāṁ āe, rāvana carana sīsa tinha nāe .
बिहसि दसानन पूँछी बाता । कहसि न सुक आपनि कुसलाता ॥
bihasi dasānana pūṁchī bātā, kahasi na suka āpani kusalātā .
पुनि कहु खबरि बिभीषन केरी । जाहि मृत्यु आई अति नेरी ॥
puni kahu khabari bibhīṣana kerī, jāhi mṛtyu āī ati nerī .
करत राज लंका सठ त्यागी । होइहि जव कर कीट अभागी ॥
karata rāja laṁkā saṭha tyāgī, hoihi java kara kīṭa abhāgī .
पुनि कहु भालु कीस कटकाई । कठिन काल प्रेरित चलि आई ॥
puni kahu bhālu kīsa kaṭakāī, kaṭhina kāla prerita cali āī .
जिन्ह के जीवन कर रखवारा । भयउ मृदुल चित सिंधु बिचारा ॥
jiṁha ke jīvana kara rakhavārā, bhayau mṛdula cita siṁdhu bicārā .
कहु तपसिन्ह कै बात बहोरी । जिन्ह के हृदयँ त्रास अति मोरी ॥
kahu tapasinha kai bāta bahorī, jinha ke hṛdayaṁ trāsa ati morī .

Bowing their head at Lakshman's feet the spies left—praising his generosity and singing the glories of the Lord. Still repeating Rāma's virtues, they arrived at Lankā and prostrated before Rāvan. The Ten-headed laughed as he enquired, "Tell me of your welfare, O Shuka; and then let me hear about Vibhishan, whom death has drawn so near. The fool left Lankā—where he was a lord—and now that wretch will be crushed as weevil along with the wheat. And tell me about these bears and monkeys who have been driven here by the fiat of their cruel fate—though I must say the poor old softhearted sea stands as a barrier and protector of their lives for now. Further tell me of those hermits whose hearts, I am sure, are filled in unrelenting fear of me.

जब तें रामु ब्याहि घर आए । नित नव मंगल मोद बधाए ॥
दीन दयाल बिरिदु संभारी । हरहु नाथ मम संकट भारी ॥
मंगल भवन अमंगल हारी । द्रवउ सो दसरथ अजिर बिहारी ॥

दोहा-*dohā:*

की भइ भेंट कि फिरि गए श्रवन सुजसु सुनि मोर ।
kī bhai bheṁṭa ki phiri gae śravana sujasu suni mora,
कहसि न रिपु दल तेज बल बहुत चकित चित तोर ॥५३॥
kahasi na ripu dala teja bala bahuta cakita cita tora. 53 .

प्रबिसि नगर कीजे सब काजा । हृदयँ राखि कोसलपुर राजा ॥
जपहिं नामु जन आरत भारी । मिटहिं कुसंकट होहिं सुखारी ॥
सियावर राम जय जय राम । मेरे प्रभु राम जय जय राम ॥

Did they meet you as suppliants? Or did they take to flight on hearing reports of my great repute and renown? Why don't you speak—tell me of the enemy, of their forces, their strength? Why, your wits seem so utterly fazed?"

चौपाई-caupāī:

नाथ कृपा करि पूँछेहु जैसें। मानहु कहा क्रोध तजि तैसें॥
nātha kṛpā kari pūm̐chehu jaiseṁ, mānahu kahā krodha taji taiseṁ .
मिला जाइ जब अनुज तुम्हारा। जातहिं राम तिलक तेहि सारा॥
milā jāi jaba anuja tumhārā, jātahiṁ rāma tilaka tehi sārā .
रावन दूत हमहि सुनि काना। कपिन्ह बाँधि दीन्हे दुख नाना॥
rāvana dūta hamahi suni kānā, kapinha bām̐dhi dīnhe dukha nānā .
श्रवन नासिका काटैं लागे। राम सपथ दीन्हें हम त्यागे॥
śravana nāsikā kāṭaiṁ lāge, rāma sapatha dīnheṁ hama tyāge .
पूँछिहु नाथ राम कटकाई। बदन कोटि सत बरनि न जाई॥
pūm̐chihu nātha rāma kaṭakāī, badana koṭi sata barani na jāī .
नाना बरन भालु कपि धारी। बिकटानन बिसाल भयकारी॥
nānā barana bhālu kapi dhārī, bikaṭānana bisāla bhayakārī .
जेहिं पुर दहेउ हतेउ सुत तोरा। सकल कपिन्ह महँ तेहि बलु थोरा॥
jehiṁ pura daheu hateu suta torā, sakala kapinha maham̐ tehi balu thorā.
अमित नाम भट कठिन कराला। अमित नाग बल बिपुल बिसाला॥
amita nāma bhaṭa kaṭhina karālā, amita nāga bala bipula bisālā .

"As you asked, O lord, do please listen in that same spirit as well; and believe as true what we are about to tell you without being angry, we pray. Soon as your brother joined him, Rāma bestowed on his forehead the sacred Tilak of sovereignty. When discovered to be your spies, we were bound and hurt in many ways by the monkeys; they were about to cut off our ears and nose, but when we invoked the name of Rāma, they let us go. You ask, my lord, of Rāma's army—but a myriad tongues would fail to describe it. It is grand battalions of bears and monkeys of diverse hues and gruesome visage, all huge and terrible. He who set fire to the city and slew your son is the very weakest of all. There are innumerable champions there—countless reputable names, all of whom are fierce and unyielding monsters of huge forms, each with strength of several elephants.

जब तें रामु ब्याहि घर आए। नित नव मंगल मोद बधाए॥
दीन दयाल बिरिदु संभारी। हरहु नाथ मम संकट भारी॥
मंगल भवन अमंगल हारी। द्रवउ सो दसरथ अजिर बिहारी॥

दोहा-*dohā:*

द्विबिद मयंद नील नल अंगद गद बिकटासि।
dvibida mayaṁda nīla nala aṁgada gada bikaṭāsi,
दधिमुख केहरि निसठ सठ जामवंत बलरासि॥५४॥
dadhimukha kehari nisaṭha saṭha jāmavaṁta balarāsi. 54 .

प्रबिसि नगर कीजे सब काजा। हृदयँ राखि कोसलपुर राजा॥
जपहिं नामु जन आरत भारी। मिटहिं कुसंकट होहिं सुखारी॥
सियावर राम जय जय राम। मेरे प्रभु राम जय जय राम॥

Dwivid and Mayand, Nīla and Nala, Aṁgad, Gada and Biktāsi; then again Dadhimukh and Kehari, Saṭha and Nisaṭha, and the powerful Jāmavaṁt—they are all repositories of untold might.

Dt: ____________________

चौपाई-*caupāī:*

ए कपि सब सुग्रीव समाना । इन्ह सम कोटिन्ह गनइ को नाना ॥
e kapi saba sugrīva samānā, inha sama koṭinha ganai ko nānā .
राम कृपाँ अतुलित बल तिन्हहीं । तृन समान त्रैलोकहि गनहीं ॥
rāma kṛpām̐ atulita bala tinhahīṁ, tṛna samāna trailokahi ganahīṁ .
अस मैं सुना श्रवन दसकंधर । पदुम अठारह जूथप बंदर ॥
asa maiṁ sunā śravana dasakaṁdhara, paduma aṭhāraha jūthapa baṁdara.
नाथ कटक महँ सो कपि नाहीं । जो न तुम्हहि जीतै रन माहीं ॥
nātha kaṭaka maham̐ so kapi nāhīṁ, jo na tumhahi jītai rana māhīṁ .
परम क्रोध मीजहिं सब हाथा । आयसु पै न देहिं रघुनाथा ॥
parama krodha mījahiṁ saba hāthā, āyasu pai na dehiṁ raghunāthā .
सोषहिं सिंधु सहित झष ब्याला । पूरहिं न त भरि कुधर बिसाला ॥
soṣahiṁ siṁdhu sahita jhaṣa byālā, pūrahiṁ na ta bhari kudhara bisālā .
मर्दि गर्द मिलवहिं दससीसा । ऐसेइ बचन कहहिं सब कीसा ॥
mardi garda milavahiṁ dasasīsā, aisei bacana kahahiṁ saba kīsā .
गर्जहिं तर्जहिं सहज असंका । मानहुँ ग्रसन चहत हहिं लंका ॥
garjahiṁ tarjahiṁ sahaja asaṁkā, mānahum̐ grasana cahata hahiṁ laṁkā .

Each of them is equal to king Sugrīv—and who could count all the tens of millions of others like them? By the grace of Shrī Rāma they are all incomparable in valor; and they reckon the three spheres of creation to be no more significant than straw. I have heard it said, O Rāvan, that just the monkey chiefs number eighteen thousand billions; and in the whole of army, my lord, there is not a single monkey who could not conquer you in battle. In dire anger they are chafing and wringing their hands: 'Why isn't Shrī Rāma ordering us to march? We will scorch the ocean dry with all its water and fish and creatures, and then we will decimate Rāvan and grind him into the dust.' With such words the monkeys are hollering with great fury. Utterly void of fear, they roar and rage—as if ready to devour Lankā in mere mouthfuls.

जब तें रामु ब्याहि घर आए । नित नव मंगल मोद बधाए ॥
दीन दयाल बिरिदु संभारी । हरहु नाथ मम संकट भारी ॥
मंगल भवन अमंगल हारी । द्रवउ सो दसरथ अजिर बिहारी ॥

दोहा-*dohā:*

सहज सूर कपि भालु सब पुनि सिर पर प्रभु राम ।
sahaja sūra kapi bhālu saba puni sira para prabhu rāma,
रावन काल कोटि कहुँ जीति सकहिं संग्राम ॥५५॥
rāvana kāla koṭi kahuṁ jīti sakahiṁ saṁgrāma. 55 .

प्रबिसि नगर कीजे सब काजा । हृदयँ राखि कोसलपुर राजा ॥
जपहिं नामु जन आरत भारी । मिटहिं कुसंकट होहिं सुखारी ॥
सियावर राम जय जय राम । मेरे प्रभु राम जय जय राम ॥

These monkeys and bears are born warriors, and moreover they have the hands of the gracious Lord Rāma upon their head. Hearken O Rāvan, they would conquer even Death itself in combat a myriad times over.

Dt: ____________________

चौपाई-*caupāī:*

राम तेज बल बुधि बिपुलाई । सेष सहस सत सकहिं न गाई ॥
rāma teja bala budhi bipulāī, seṣa sahasa sata sakahiṁ na gāī .
सक सर एक सोषि सत सागर । तव भ्रातहि पूँछेउ नय नागर ॥
saka sara eka soṣi sata sāgara, tava bhrātahi pūm̐cheu naya nāgara .
तासु बचन सुनि सागर पाहीं । मागत पंथ कृपा मन माहीं ॥
tāsu bacana suni sāgara pāhīṁ, māgata paṁtha kṛpā mana māhīṁ .
सुनत बचन बिहसा दससीसा । जौं असि मति सहाय कृत कीसा ॥
sunata bacana bihasā dasasīsā, jauṁ asi mati sahāya kṛta kīsā .
सहज भीरु कर बचन दृढ़ाई । सागर सन ठानी मचलाई ॥
sahaja bhīru kara bacana dṛṛhāī, sāgara sana ṭhānī macalāī .
मूढ़ मृषा का करसि बड़ाई । रिपु बल बुद्धि थाह मैं पाई ॥
mūṛha mṛṣā kā karasi baṛāī, ripu bala buddhi thāha maiṁ pāī .
सचिव सभीत बिभीषन जाकें । बिजय बिभूति कहाँ जग ताकें ॥
saciva sabhīta bibhīṣana jākeṁ, bijaya bibhūti kahām̐ jaga tākeṁ .
सुनि खल बचन दूत रिस बाढ़ी । समय बिचारि पत्रिका काढ़ी ॥
suni khala bacana dūta risa bāṛhī, samaya bicāri patrikā kāṛhī .
रामानुज दीन्ही यह पाती । नाथ बचाइ जुड़ावहु छाती ॥
rāmānuja dīnhī yaha pātī, nātha bacāi juṛāvahu chātī .
बिहसि बाम कर लीन्ही रावन । सचिव बोलि सठ लाग बचावन ॥
bihasi bāma kara līnhī rāvana, saciva boli saṭha lāga bacāvana .

And as for Him, a hundred thousand Sheshas would fail to describe the valor, might, wisdom and majesty of Shri Rāma. With a single shaft he can burn up a hundred seas; and yet, being a master of propriety, he sought the advice of your brother and in accordance with his suggestion he repaired to the sea and humbly asks the favor of a passage through." The Ten-headed laughed to hear these words, "Truly it was because of such a mindset that he took the monkeys for his allies; and that is why, putting faith in the advice of my brother—who's a born coward—he insists on badgering the ocean for the impossible—so childlike. Why do you shower sham praises upon them, fool? Enough! I have fathomed the extent of the enemy's strength and their skills. Who in the world can achieve any glory or triumph who has such cowardly counselors as Vibhishan?" The envoys waxed angry to hear the words of the wicked monarch, and decided that it was the right moment to produce the missive given by Lakshman. "Rāma's brother gave us this letter, O lord; please have it read, and may it soothe your heart." Rāvan laughed as he took the letter in his left hand. Then summoning a minister, the fool asked for the letter to be read out aloud—and the letter said:

दोहा-*dohā:*

बातन्ह मनहि रिझाइ सठ जनि घालसि कुल खीस।
bātanha manahi rijhāi saṭha jani ghālasi kula khīsa,
राम बिरोध न उबरसि सरन बिष्नु अज ईस ॥५६क॥
rāma birodha na ubarasi sarana biṣṇu aja īsa. 56(ka) .

की तजि मान अनुज इव प्रभु पद पंकज भृंग।
kī taji māna anuja iva prabhu pada paṁkaja bhṛṁga,
होहि कि राम सरानल खल कुल सहित पतंग ॥५६ख॥
hohi ki rāma sarānala khala kula sahita pataṁga. 56(kha) .

"Stop living on mere talks and flattering words, you fool, and be not the one who causes the destruction of his entire race. If you are opposed to Rāma, you will not be saved even though Vishnu, Brahmma, and Shiva be your protectors. Abandon all pride and, like your brother, fly like a bee to the lotus feet of the Lord, or like a moth you will be consumed—you and your entire clan—in the flames of Shrī Rāma's fiery shafts."

Dt: ______________________

चौपाई-*caupāī:*

सुनत सभय मन मुख मुसुकाई । कहत दसानन सबहि सुनाई ॥
sunata sabhaya mana mukha musukāī, kahata dasānana sabahi sunāī .
भूमि परा कर गहत अकासा । लघु तापस कर बाग बिलासा ॥
bhūmi parā kara gahata akāsā, laghu tāpasa kara bāga bilāsā .
कह सुक नाथ सत्य सब बानी । समुझहु छाड़ि प्रकृति अभिमानी ॥
kaha suka nātha satya saba bānī, samujhahu chāṛi prakṛti abhimānī .
सुनहु बचन मम परिहरि क्रोधा । नाथ राम सन तजहु बिरोधा ॥
sunahu bacana mama parihari krodhā, nātha rāma sana tajahu birodhā .
अति कोमल रघुबीर सुभाऊ । जद्यपि अखिल लोक कर राऊ ॥
ati komala raghubīra subhāū, jadyapi akhila loka kara rāū .
मिलत कृपा तुम्ह पर प्रभु करिही । उर अपराध न एकउ धरिही ॥
milata kṛpā tumha para prabhu karihī, ura aparādha na ekau dharihī .
जनकसुता रघुनाथहि दीजे । एतना कहा मोर प्रभु कीजे ॥
janakasutā raghunāthahi dīje, etanā kahā mora prabhu kīje .
जब तेहिं कहा देन बैदेही । चरन प्रहार कीन्ह सठ तेही ॥
jaba tehiṁ kahā dena baidehī, carana prahāra kīnha saṭha tehī .
नाइ चरन सिरु चला सो तहाँ । कृपासिंधु रघुनायक जहाँ ॥
nāi carana siru calā so tahāṁ, kṛpāsiṁdhu raghunāyaka jahāṁ .
करि प्रनामु निज कथा सुनाई । राम कृपाँ आपनि गति पाई ॥
kari pranāmu nija kathā sunāī, rāma kṛpāṁ āpani gati pāī .
रिषि अगस्ति कीं साप भवानी । राछस भयउ रहा मुनि ग्यानी ॥
riṣi agasti kīṁ sāpa bhavānī, rāchasa bhayau rahā muni gyānī .
बंदि राम पद बारहिं बारा । मुनि निज आश्रम कहुँ पगु धारा ॥
baṁdi rāma pada bārahiṁ bārā, muni nija āśrama kahuṁ pagu dhārā .

Rāvan was terror-stricken at heart but making a show of bravado he feigned a smile and spoke aloud for all to hear, "The younger hermit's eloquence is like a man lying on ground, trying to clutch with his hands the vaults of heavens." The envoy Shuka spoke again: "My lord, take every word of this message to be true; be wise and abandon your innate arrogance. Cease from wrath and hearken to our advice: please make an end, O sire, of your feud with Rāma. Raghubīr is exceedingly kind, though he is the Sovereign of the entire universe. The Lord will be gracious to you directly as you approach him, and he will not take to his heart even a single offence of yours. Restore to him Janak's daughter—this sire is all we ask of you; pray do so."

दोहा-dohā:

बिनय न मानत जलधि जड़ गए तीनि दिन बीति ।
binaya na mānata jaladhi jaṛa gae tīni dina bīti,
बोले राम सकोप तब भय बिनु होइ न प्रीति ॥५७॥
bole rāma sakopa taba bhaya binu hoi na prīti. 57 .

When Shuka spoke to Rāvan about returning Sītā, the wretch kicked at him with his foot. After bowing to Rāvan's feet, Shuka too went to meet the All-merciful Rāma; and there making obeisance to the Lord, he told all about himself; and then by Rāma's favor he recovered his original state. Shuka was an enlightened sage, and it was by Agastya's curse, O Bhavānī, that he had been transformed into a demon. Adoring Shrī Rāma's feet again and again, the sage returned to his hermitage.

Meanwhile, although three days had passed, the immoveable ocean would make no answer to the Lord's prayers. Thereupon Shrī Rāma spoke with fury, "Looks like affinity, bond, kinship does not arise without some underlying awe and fear.

चौपाई-*caupāī:*

लछिमन बान सरासन आनू । सोषौं बारिधि बिसिख कृसानू ॥
lachimana bāna sarāsana ānū, soṣaum̐ bāridhi bisikha kṛsānū .
सठ सन बिनय कुटिल सन प्रीती । सहज कृपन सन सुंदर नीती ॥
saṭha sana binaya kuṭila sana prītī, sahaja kṛpana sana suṁdara nītī .
ममता रत सन ग्यान कहानी । अति लोभी सन बिरति बखानी ॥
mamatā rata sana gyāna kahānī, ati lobhī sana birati bakhānī .
क्रोधिहि सम कामिहि हरि कथा । ऊसर बीज बएँ फल जथा ॥
krodhihi sama kāmihi hari kathā, ūsara bīja baem̐ phala jathā .
अस कहि रघुपति चाप चढ़ावा । यह मत लछिमन के मन भावा ॥
asa kahi raghupati cāpa caṛhāvā, yaha mata lachimana ke mana bhāvā .
संघानेउ प्रभु बिसिख कराला । उठी उदधि उर अंतर ज्वाला ॥
saṁghāneu prabhu bisikha karālā, uṭhī udadhi ura aṁtara jvālā .
मकर उरग झष गन अकुलाने । जरत जंतु जलनिधि जब जाने ॥
makara uraga jhaṣa gana akulāne, jarata jaṁtu jalanidhi jaba jāne .
कनक थार भरि मनि गन नाना । बिप्र रूप आयउ तजि माना ॥
kanaka thāra bhari mani gana nānā, bipra rūpa āyau taji mānā .

Lakshman bring at once my bow and arrows, and with one fiery shaft I shall dry up the ocean. To offer supplications to a barbarian, to lavish affections upon a rogue, to dispense policy of universal goodness upon a born miser, to teach wisdom to one entangled in worldliness, to glorify detachment in front of the covetous, to lecture on equanimity before an irascible person, and to tell of God unto a libidinous man—these are all the same as sowing seeds in a barren field." Saying so Rāma strung up his bow and this act pleased Lakshman greatly. When the Lord fitted the terrible arrow to his bow, a burning ensued in the heart of the ocean and crocodiles, serpents, fishes, creature all seemed thrown into dire straits. When the Ocean perceived that all its inhabitants were singeing, he presented himself in all humility before the Lord taking the form of a Brahmin, and he brought out as gift a golden receptacle filled with every kind of jewel.

दोहा-dohā:

काटेहिं पइ कदरी फरइ कोटि जतन कोउ सींच ।
kāṭehiṁ pai kadarī pharai koṭi jatana kou sīṁca,
बिनय न मान खगेस सुनु डाटेहिं पइ नव नीच ॥५८॥
binaya na māna khagesa sunu ḍāṭehiṁ pai nava nīca. 58 .

Though one may take infinite pains in watering a plantain, yet it will not bear fruit unless it is hewed. Likewise, O king of birds, [continued Kak-Bhushundi], a mean upstart heeds neither prayer nor compliment, but yields only to reprimand.

Dt: ____________________

चौपाई-caupāī:

सभय सिंधु गहि पद प्रभु केरे । छमहु नाथ सब अवगुन मेरे ॥
sabhaya siṁdhu gahi pada prabhu kere, chamahu nātha saba avaguna mere.

गगन समीर अनल जल धरनी । इन्ह कइ नाथ सहज जड़ करनी ॥
gagana samīra anala jala dharanī, inha kai nātha sahaja jaṛa karanī.

तव प्रेरित मायाँ उपजाए । सृष्टि हेतु सब ग्रंथनि गाए ॥
tava prerita māyām̐ upajāe, sṛṣṭi hetu saba graṁthani gāe.

प्रभु आयसु जेहि कहँ जस अहई । सो तेहि भाँति रहें सुख लहई ॥
prabhu āyasu jehi kaham̐ jasa ahaī, so tehi bhām̐ti raheṁ sukha lahaī.

प्रभु भल कीन्ह मोहि सिख दीन्ही । मरजादा पुनि तुम्हरी कीन्ही ॥
prabhu bhala kīnha mohi sikha dīnhī, marajādā puni tumharī kīnhī.

ढोल गवाँर सूद्र पसु नारी । सकल ताड़ना के अधिकारी ॥
ḍhola gavām̐ra sūdra pasu nārī, sakala tāṛanā ke adhikārī.

प्रभु प्रताप मैं जाब सुखाई । उतरिहि कटकु न मोरि बड़ाई ॥
prabhu pratāpa maiṁ jāba sukhāī, utarihi kaṭaku na mori baṛāī.

प्रभु अग्या अपेल श्रुति गाई । करौं सो बेगि जो तुम्हहि सोहाई ॥
prabhu agyā apela śruti gāī, karauṁ so begi jo tumhahi sohāī.

The terrified ocean clasped the Lord's feet, pleading: "Pardon, O Lord, all my offences. The ether, air, fire, water, and earth are naturally dull and slow to change. It is your Māyā which has spun everything out—to lend visibility to your Creation—as all the scriptures declare; and like each has been ordained by the Lord's Will, likewise it must act out—to retain its well-being. My lord has done well in giving me this lesson—but still it was you who first fixed my natural bounds. A drum, a rustic, a workman, a beastly woman—all these deserve instructions. No doubt, by the Lord's might I shall be dried up and the army will cross over, but that will bring little glory to me. Thy command is inviolable—so declare the Vedas; hence I shall immediately do whatever pleases Thee."

जब तें रामु ब्याहि घर आए । नित नव मंगल मोद बधाए ॥
दीन दयाल बिरिदु संभारी । हरहु नाथ मम संकट भारी ॥
मंगल भवन अमंगल हारी । द्रवउ सो दसरथ अजिर बिहारी ॥

दोहा-*dohā:*

सुनत बिंनीत बचन अति कह कृपाल मुसुकाइ ।
sunata binīta bacana ati kaha kṛpāla musukāi,
जेहि बिधि उतरै कपि कटकु तात सो कहहु उपाइ ॥५९॥
jehi bidhi utarai kapi kaṭaku tāta so kahahu upāi. 59 .

प्रबिसि नगर कीजे सब काजा । हृदयँ राखि कोसलपुर राजा ॥
जपहिं नामु जन आरत भारी । मिटहिं कुसंकट होहिं सुखारी ॥
सियावर राम जय जय राम । मेरे प्रभु राम जय जय राम ॥

Upon hearing his exceedingly humble speech, the All-merciful smiled and spoke, “Tell me dear of some device whereby these monkeys may cross over to the other side.”

चौपाई-*caupāī:*

नाथ नील नल कपि द्वौ भाई । लरिकाईं रिषि आसिष पाई ॥
nātha nīla nala kapi dvau bhāī, larikāīṁ riṣi āsiṣa pāī .
तिन्ह कें परस किएँ गिरि भारे । तरिहहिं जलधि प्रताप तुम्हारे ॥
tinha keṁ parasa kieṁ giri bhāre, tarihahiṁ jaladhi pratāpa tumhāre .
मैं पुनि उर धरि प्रभु प्रभुताई । करिहउँ बल अनुमान सहाई ॥
maiṁ puni ura dhari prabhu prabhutāī, karihauṁ bala anumāna sahāī .
एहि बिधि नाथ पयोधि बँधाइअ । जेहिं यह सुजसु लोक तिहुँ गाइअ ॥
ehi bidhi nātha payodhi baṁdhāia, jehiṁ yaha sujasu loka tihuṁ gāia .
एहिं सर मम उत्तर तट बासी । हतहु नाथ खल नर अघ रासी ॥
ehiṁ sara mama uttara taṭa bāsī, hatahu nātha khala nara agha rāsī .
सुनि कृपाल सागर मन पीरा । तुरतहिं हरी राम रनधीरा ॥
suni kṛpāla sāgara mana pīrā, turatahiṁ harī rāma ranadhīrā .
देखि राम बल पौरुष भारी । हरषि पयोनिधि भयउ सुखारी ॥
dekhi rāma bala pauruṣa bhārī, haraṣi payonidhi bhayau sukhārī .
सकल चरित कहि प्रभुहि सुनावा । चरन बंदि पाथोधि सिधावा ॥
sakala carita kahi prabhuhi sunāvā, carana baṁdi pāthodhi sidhāvā .

“My lord, there are two monkey brothers, Nīla and Nala, who as children were blessed by a sage and as a result even the mightiest rocks touched by them will float upon water—by dint of your grace. And cherishing my Lord’s greatness in the heart, I too shall assist to the best of my ability. In this manner, O Lord, have the ocean bridged, so that this glorious deed of yours may be sung in all the three spheres of Creation for all times. Since your arrow is already drawn, let it fly to slay the vile criminals dwelling on my northern shore.” On hearing that Shrī Rāma, who is as tender-hearted as he is staunch in battle, at once discharged the arrow to relieve the agony of the Ocean’s heart; and at the sight of his outstanding valor and might the Ocean rejoiced and became easy of mind; and after recounting to the Lord of all that had transpired took his permission to leave, bowing to the feet of the Lord.

छंद-*chamda:*

निज भवन गवनेउ सिंधु श्रीरघुपतिहि यह मत भायऊ ।

nija bhavana gavaneu siṁdhu śrīraghupatihi yaha mata bhāyaū,

यह चरित कलि मलहर जथामति दास तुलसी गायऊ ॥

yaha carita kali malahara jathāmati dāsa tulasī gāyaū .

सुख भवन संसय समन दवन बिषाद रघुपति गुन गना ।

sukha bhavana saṁsaya samana davana biṣāda raghupati guna ganā,

तजि सकल आस भरोस गावहि सुनहि संतत सठ मना ॥

taji sakala āsa bharosa gāvahi sunahi saṁtata saṭha manā .

With his counsel having met the approval of the Lord, the Ocean returned to his elements. This episode of Shrī Rāma, which wipes out all impurities of this Kali-Yuga, was sung to the best of his ability by Tulsīdās. The excellencies of Raghupati are treasures of delight, a panacea for all doubts, and the very unfailing remedies for sorrows. O mind, give up every other hope and faith, and ever sing and hear the glories of the Lord-God Shrī Rāma.

दोहा-dohā:

सकल सुमंगल दायक रघुनायक गुन गान ।
sakala sumaṁgala dāyaka raghunāyaka guna gāna,
सादर सुनहिं ते तरहिं भव सिंधु बिना जलजान ॥६०॥
sādara sunahiṁ te tarahiṁ bhava siṁdhu binā jalajāna. 60 .

A recital of the virtues of Shrī Rāma, Lord of Raghus, is the perennial fount of every blessing; and they who reverently hear them, cross this ocean of worldly existence without a need of any other bark.

जब तें रामु ब्याहि घर आए । नित नव मंगल मोद बधाए ॥
दीन दयाल बिरिदु संभारी । हरहु नाथ मम संकट भारी ॥
मंगल भवन अमंगल हारी । द्रवउ सो दसरथ अजिर बिहारी ॥

इति श्रीमद्रामचरितमानसे सकलकलिकलुषविध्वंसने

iti śrīmadrāmacaritamānase sakalakalikaluṣavidhvaṁsane

पञ्चमः सोपानः सुन्दरकाण्ड

pañcamaḥ sopānaḥ sundarakāṇḍa

श्रीरामचरणार्पणमस्तु

śrī rāma caraṇāarpaṇamastu

कायेन वाचा मनसेन्द्रियैर्वा बुद्ध्यात्मना वा प्रकृतेः स्वभावात् ।

kāyena vācā manasendriyairvā buddhyātmanā vā prakṛteḥ svabhāvāt,

करोमि यद्यत्सकलं परस्मै नारायणयेति समर्पयामि ॥

karomi yadyatsakalaṁ parasmai nārāyaṇayeti samarpayāmi.

Sundarakānda,
the Fifth-Ascent into the Mānasa Lake of Shrī Rāma's Charita,
which eradicates all the impurities of the Kali-Yuga,
is hereby dedicated to
the Lotus Feet of theLord-God Shrī Rāma

Whatever it is I do – through body, mind, speech, or sense-organs,
or with my intellect and soul,
or with my innate natural tendencies, whatever it be:
I offer it all to Shrī Rāma

प्रबिसि नगर कीजे सब काजा । हृदयँ राखि कोसलपुर राजा ॥
जपहिं नामु जन आरत भारी । मिटहिं कुसंकट होहिं सुखारी ॥
सियावर राम जय जय राम । मेरे प्रभु राम जय जय राम ॥

Dt: ____________________

श्री हनुमान चालीसा — śrī hanumāna cālīsā

दोहा - dohā

श्रीगुरु चरन सरोज रज निज मन मुकुर सुधारि । बरनऊँ रघुबर बिमल जस जो दायक फल चारि ॥
śrīguru carana saroja raja nija mana mukura sudhāri, baranaūṁ raghubara bimala jasa jo dāyaka phala cāri.

बुद्धि हीन तनु जानिकै सुमिरौं पवन कुमार । बल बुद्धि बिद्या देहु मोहि हरहु कलेश विकार ॥
buddhi hīna tanu jānikai sumiraum̐ pavana kumāra, bala buddhi bidyā dehu mohi harahu kaleśa vikāra.

चौपाई - caupāī

जय हनुमान ज्ञान गुण सागर । जय कपीश तिहुँ लोक उजागर ॥ 1
jaya hanumāna jñāna guṇa sāgara, jaya kapīśa tihum̐ loka ujāgara.

राम दूत अतुलित बल धामा । अंजनिपुत्र पवनसुत नामा ॥ 2
rāma dūta atulita bala dhāmā, aṁjaniputra pavanasuta nāmā.

महाबीर बिक्रम बजरंगी । कुमति निवार सुमति के संगी ॥ 3
mahābīra bikrama bajaraṁgī, kumati nivāra sumati ke saṁgī.

कंचन बरन बिराज सुबेषा । कानन कुंडल कुंचित केशा ॥ 4
kaṁcana barana birāja subeṣā, kānana kuṁḍala kuṁcita keśā.

हाथ बज्र और ध्वजा बिराजै । काँधे मूँज जनेऊ साजै ॥ 5
hātha bajra aura dhvajā birājai, kām̐dhe mūm̐ja janeū sājai.

शङ्कर स्वयं केशरीनन्दन । तेज प्रताप महा जग बंदन ॥ 6
śaṅkara svayaṁ keśarīnaṁdana, teja pratāpa mahā jaga baṁdana.

विद्यावान गुणी अति चातुर । राम काज करिबे को आतुर ॥ 7
vidyāvāna guṇī ati cātura, rāma kāja karibe ko ātura.

प्रभु चरित्र सुनिबे को रसिया । राम लखन सीता मन बसिया ॥ 8
prabhu caritra sunibe ko rasiyā, rāma lakhana sītā mana basiyā.

सूक्ष्म रूप धरि सियहिं दिखावा । बिकट रूप धरि लंक जरावा ॥ 9
sūkṣma rūpa dhari siyahiṁ dikhāvā, bikaṭa rūpa dhari laṁka jarāvā.

भीम रूप धरि असुर सँहारे । रामचन्द्र के काज सँवारे ॥ 10
bhīma rūpa dhari asura sam̐hāre, rāmacandra ke kāja sam̐vāre.

लाय संजीवनि लखन जियाये । श्री रघुबीर हरषि उर लाये ॥ 11
lāya saṁjīvani lakhana jiyāye, śrī raghubīra haraṣi ura lāye.

रघुपति कीन्ही बहुत बडाई । तुम मम प्रिय भरतहि सम भाई ॥ 12
raghupati kīnhī bahuta baṛāī, tuma mama priya bharatahiṁ sama bhāī.

सहस बदन तुम्हरो जस गावैं । अस कहि श्रीपति कंठ लगावैं ॥ 13
sahasa badana tumharo jasa gāvaiṁ, asa kahi śrīpati kaṁṭha lagāvaiṁ.

सनकादिक ब्रह्मादि मुनीशा । नारद शारद सहित अहीशा ॥ 14
sanakādika brahmādi munīśā, nārada śārada sahita ahīśā.

जम कुबेर दिगपाल जहाँ ते । कबि कोबिद कहि सकै कहाँ ते ॥ 15
jama kubera digapāla jahām̐ te, kabi kobida kahi sakai kahām̐ te.

तुम उपकार सुग्रीवहिं कीन्हा । राम मिलाय राज पद दीन्हा ॥ 16
tuma upakāra sugrīvahiṁ kīnhā, rāma milāya rāja pada dīnhā.

तुम्हरो मंत्र बिभीषन माना । लंकेश्वर भए सब जग जाना ॥ 17
tumharo maṁtra bibhīṣana mānā, laṁkeśvara bhae saba jaga jānā.

जुग सहस्र जोजन पर भानू । लील्यो ताहि मधुर फल जानू ॥ 18
juga sahastra jojana para bhānū, līlyo tāhi madhura phala jānū.

प्रभु मुद्रिका मेलि मुख माहीं । जलधि लाँघि गये अचरज नाहीं ॥ 19
prabhu mudrikā meli mukha māhīṁ, jaladhi lām̐ghi gaye acaraja nāhīṁ.

दुर्गम काज जगत के जेते । सुगम अनुग्रह तुम्हरे तेते ॥ 20
durgama kāja jagata ke jete, sugama anugraha tumhare tete.

राम दुआरे तुम रखवारे । होत न आज्ञा बिनु पैसारे ॥ 21
rāma duāre tuma rakhavāre, hota na ājñā binu paisāre.

सब सुख लहैं तुम्हारी शरना । तुम रक्षक काहू को डर ना ॥ 22
saba sukha lahaiṁ tumhārī śaranā, tuma rakṣaka kāhū ko ḍara nā.

आपन तेज सम्हारो आपै । तीनों लोक हाँक ते काँपै ॥ 23
āpana teja samhāro āpai, tīnauṁ loka hām̐ka te kām̐pai.

भूत पिशाच निकट नहिं आवै । महाबीर जब नाम सुनावै ॥ 24
bhūta piśāca nikaṭa nahiṁ āvai, mahābīra jaba nāma sunāvai.

नासै रोग हरै सब पीरा । जपत निरंतर हनुमत बीरा ॥ 25
nāsai roga harai saba pīrā, japata niraṁtara hanumata bīrā.

संकट ते हनुमान छुडावै । मन क्रम बचन ध्यान जो लावै ॥ 26
saṁkaṭa te hanumāna chuṛavai, mana krama bacana dhyāna jo lāvai.

सब पर राम तपस्वी राजा । तिन के काज सकल तुम साजा ॥ 27
saba para rāma tapasvī rājā, tina ke kāja sakala tuma sājā.

और मनोरथ जो कोउ लावै । तासु अमित जीवन फल पावै ॥ 28
aura manoratha jo kou lāvai, tāsu amita jīvana phala pāvai.

चारों जुग परताप तुम्हारा । है परसिद्ध जगत उजियारा ॥ 29
cārauṁ juga paratāpa tumhārā, hai parasiddha jagata ujiyārā.

साधु संत के तुम रखवारे । असुर निकंदन राम दुलारे ॥ 30
sādhu saṁta ke tuma rakhavāre, asura nikaṁdana rāma dulāre.

अष्ट सिद्धि नव निधि के दाता । अस बर दीन्ह जानकी माता ॥ 31
aṣṭa siddhi nava nidhi ke dātā, asa bara dīnha jānakī mātā.

राम रसायन तुम्हरे पासा । सदा रहउ रघुपति के दासा ॥ 32
rāma rasāyana tumhare pāsā, sadā rahau raghupati ke dāsā.

तुम्हरे भजन राम को पावै । जनम जनम के दुख बिसरावै ॥ 33
tumhare bhajana rāma ko pāvai, janama janama ke dukha bisarāvai.

अंत काल रघुबर पुर जाई । जहाँ जन्म हरिभक्त कहाई ॥ 34
aṁta kāla raghubara pura jāī, jahām̐ janma haribhakta kahāī.

और देवता चित्त न धरई । हनुमत सेइ सर्ब सुख करई ॥ 35
aura devatā citta na dharaī, hanumata sei sarba sukha karaī.

संकट कटै मिटै सब पीरा । जो सुमिरै हनुमत बलबीरा ॥ 36
saṁkaṭa kaṭai miṭai saba pīrā, jo sumirai hanumata balabīrā.

जय जय जय हनुमान गोसाईं । कृपा करहु गुरु देव की नाईं ॥ 37
jaya jaya jaya hanumāna gosāīṁ, kṛpā karahu guru deva kī nāīṁ.

यह शत बार पाठ कर जोई । छूटै बंदि महा सुख सोई ॥ 38
yaha śata bāra pāṭha kara joī, chūṭai baṁdi mahā sukha soī.

जो यह पढ़ै हनुमान चालीसा । होय सिद्धि साखी गौरीसा ॥ 39
jo yaha paṛhai hanumāna cālīsā, hoya siddhi sākhī gaurīsā.

तुलसीदास सदा हरि चेरा । कीजै नाथ हृदय महँ डेरा ॥ 40
tulasīdāsa sadā hari cerā, kījai nātha hṛdaya maham̐ ḍerā.

दोहा - dohā

पवन तनय संकट हरन मंगल मूरति रूप । राम लखन सीता सहित हृदय बसहु सुर भूप ॥
pavana tanaya saṁkaṭa harana maṁgala mūrati rūpa, rāma lakhana sītā sahita hṛdaya basahu sura bhūpa.

श्री रामायण आरती — śrī rāmāyaṇa ārati

आरति श्रीरामायनजी की । कीरति कलित ललित सिय पी की ॥
ārati śrīrāmāyanajī kī, kīrati kalita lalita siya pī kī.

गावत ब्रह्मादिक मुनि नारद । बालमीक बिग्यान बिसारद ॥
gāvata brahmādika muni nārada, bālamīka bigyāna bisārada.
सुक सनकादि सेष अरु सारद । बरनि पवनसुत कीरति नीकी ॥ १ ॥
suka sanakādi seṣa aru sārada, barani pavanasuta kīrati nīkī. [1]

गावत बेद पुरान अष्टदस । छओ सास्त्र सब ग्रंथन को रस ॥
gāvata beda purāna aṣṭadasa, chao sāstra saba gramthana ko rasa.
मुनि जन धन संतन को सरबस । सार अंस संमत सबही की ॥ २ ॥
muni jana dhana saṁtana ko sarabasa, sāra aṁsa saṁmata sabahī kī. [2]

गावत संतत संभु भवानी । अरु घटसंभव मुनि बिग्यानी ॥
gāvata saṁtata saṁbhu bhavānī, aru ghaṭasaṁbhava muni bigyānī.
ब्यास आदि कबिबर्ज बखानी । कागभुसुंडि गरुड के ही की ॥ ३ ॥
byāsa ādi kabibarja bakhānī, kāgabhusuṁḍi garuḍa ke hī kī. [3]

कलिमल हरनि बिषय रस फीकी । सुभग सिंगार मुक्ति जुबती की ॥
kalimala harani biṣaya rasa phīkī, subhaga siṁgāra mukti jubatī kī.
दलन रोग भव मूरि अमी की । तात मात सब बिधि तुलसी की ॥ ४ ॥
dalana roga bhava mūri amī kī, tāta māta saba bidhi tulasī kī. [4]

आरति श्रीरामायनजी की । कीरति कलित ललित सिय पी की ...
ārati śrīrāmāyanajī kī, kīrati kalita lalita siya pī kī ...

श्री हनुमान आरती — śrī hanumāna āratī

आरती कीजै हनुमान लला की । दुष्ट-दलन रघुनाथ कला की ॥ 1
āratī kījai hanumāna lalā kī, duṣṭa-dalana raghunātha kalā kī.
जाके बल से गिरिवर काँपै । रोग दोष जाके निकट न झाँपै ॥ 2
jāke bala se girivara kām̐pai, roga doṣa jāke nikaṭa na jhām̐pai.
अंजनि-पुत्र महा बल दाई । संतन के प्रभु सदा सहाई ॥ 3
aṁjani-putra mahā bala dāī, saṁtana ke prabhu sadā sahāī.
दे बीरा रघुनाथ पठाये । लंका जारि सीय सुधि लाये ॥ 4
de bīrā raghunātha paṭhāye, laṁkā jāri sīya sudhi lāye.
लंका-सो कोट समुद्र-सी खाई । जात पवनसुत बार न लाई ॥ 5
laṁkā-so koṭa samudra-sī khāī, jāta pavanasuta bāra na lāī.
लंका जारि असुर संहारे । सियारामजी के काज सँवारे ॥ 6
laṁkā jāri asura saṁhāre, siyārāmajī ke kāja sam̐vāre.
लछिमन मूर्छित पड़े सकारे । आनि सजीवन प्रान उबारे ॥ 7
lachimana mūrchita paṛe sakāre, āni sajīvana prāna ubāre.
पैठी पताल तोरि जम-कारे । अहिरावन की भुजा उखारे ॥ 8
paiṭhī patāla tori jama-kāre, ahirāvana kī bhujā ukhāre.
बायें भुजा असुरदल मारे । दहिने भुजा संतजन तारे ॥ 9
bāyeṁ bhujā asuradala māre, dahine bhujā saṁtajana tāre.
सुर नर मुनि आरती उतारे । जै जै जै हनुमान उचारे ॥ 10
sura nara muni āratī utāre, jai jai jai hanumāna ucāre.
कंचन थार कपूर लौ छाई । आरति करत अंजना माई ॥ 11
kaṁcana thāra kapūra lau chāī, ārati karata aṁjanā māī.
जो हनुमानजी की आरति गावै । बसि बैकुंठ परमपद पावै ॥ 12
jo hanumānajī kī ārati gāvai, basi baikuṁṭha paramapada pāvai.

आरती कीजै हनुमान लला की । दुष्ट-दलन रघुनाथ कला की ...
āratī kījai hanumāna lalā kī, duṣṭa-dalana raghunātha kalā kī ...

सियावर रामचन्द्र की जय
siyāvara rāmacandra kī jaya
पवनसुत हनुमान की जय
pavanasuta hanumāna kī jaya
गोस्वामी तुलसीदास की जय
gosvāmī tulasīdāsa kī jaya

—— Please check out our other books ——
Below is reproduced from **Tulsi Ramayana, Hindu Holy Book, by Baldev Prasad Saxena.**

ISBNs: 978-1-945739-01-9 (Paperback) / 978-1-945739-03-3 (Hardback)

(Excerpts shown below are in reduced font-size)

[Below are the beginning verses of Tulsi Rāmāyana]

शलोक-*śloka:*

वर्णानामर्थसंघानां रसानां छन्दसामपि ।
varṇānāmarthasaṁghānāṁ rasānāṁ chandasāmapi,
मङ्गलानां च कर्त्तारौ वन्दे वाणीविनायकौ ॥१॥
maṅgalānāṁ ca karttārau vande vāṇīvināyakau. 1.

Trans:

I venerate Vānī and Vināyak, the originators of the alphabet and of the multitudinous expressions of those letters; the creators of the poetic styles, of cadence, of metre; and the begetters of all blessings.

भवानीशङ्करौ वन्दे श्रद्धाविश्वासरूपिणौ ।
bhavānīśaṅkarau vande śraddhāviśvāsarūpiṇau,
याभ्यां विना न पश्यन्ति सिद्धाःस्वान्तःस्थमीश्वरम् ॥२॥
yābhyāṁ vinā na paśyanti siddhāḥsvāntaḥsthamīśvaram. 2.

Trans:

I reverence Bhawānī and Shankar, the embodiments of reverence and faith, without whom, not even the adept may see the Great Spirit which is enshrined in their very own hearts.

वन्दे बोधमयं नित्यं गुरुं शङ्कररूपिणम् ।
vande bodhamayaṁ nityaṁ guruṁ śaṅkararūpiṇam,
यमाश्रितो हि वक्रोऽपि चन्द्रः सर्वत्र वन्द्यते ॥३॥
yamāśrito hi vakro'pi candraḥ sarvatra vandyate. 3.

Trans:

I make obeisance to the eternal preceptor in the form of Shankar, who is all wisdom, and resting on whose crest the crescent moon, though crooked in shape, is everywhere honored.

सीतारामगुणग्रामपुण्यारण्यविहारिणौ ।
sītārāmaguṇagrāmapuṇyāraṇyavihāriṇau,
वन्दे विशुद्धविज्ञानौ कवीश्वरकपीश्वरौ ॥४॥
vande viśuddhavijñānau kavīśvarakapīśvarau. 4.

Trans:

I reverence the king of bards (Vālmikī) and the king of monkeys (Hanumān), of pure intelligence, who ever linger with delight in the holy woods in the shape of glories of Sītā-Rāma.

उद्भवस्थितिसंहारकारिणीं क्लेशहारिणीम् ।
udbhavasthitisaṁhārakāriṇīṁ kleśahāriṇīm,
सर्वश्रेयस्करीं सीतां नतोऽहं रामवल्लभाम् ॥५॥
sarvaśreyaskarīṁ sītāṁ nato'haṁ rāmavallabhām. 5.

Trans:

I bow to Sītā—the beloved consort of Rāma—She who's the responsible cause of creation, sustenance and dissolution of the universe—She who removes all afflictions and begets every blessing.

यन्मायावशवर्त्ति विश्वमखिलं ब्रह्मादिदेवासुरा
yanmāyāvaśavartti viśvamakhilaṁ brahmādidevāsurā
यत्सत्त्वादमृषैव भाति सकलं रज्जौ यथाहेर्भ्रमः ।
yatsattvādamṛṣaiva bhāti sakalaṁ rajjau yathāherbhramaḥ,
यत्पादप्लवमेकमेव हि भवाम्भोधेस्तितीर्षावतां
yatpādaplavamekameva hi bhavāmbhodhestitīrṣāvatāṁ
वन्देऽहं तमशेषकारणपरं रामाख्यमीशं हरिम् ॥६॥
vande'haṁ tamaśeṣakāraṇaparaṁ rāmākhyamīśaṁ harim. 6.

Trans:

I reverence Lord Harī, known by the name of Shrī Rāma—the Supreme causative Cause—whose Māyā holds sway over the entire universe, upon every being and supernatural beings from Brahmmā downwards—whose presence lends positive reality to the world of appearances: just as the false notion of serpent is imagined in a rope—and whose feet are the only bark for those eager to cross this worldly ocean of existence.

नानापुराणनिगमागमसम्मतं यद्
nānāpurāṇanigamāgamasammataṁ yad
रामायणे निगदितं क्वचिदन्यतोऽपि ।
rāmāyaṇe nigaditaṁ kvacidanyato'pi,
स्वान्तःसुखाय तुलसी रघुनाथगाथा-
svāntaḥsukhāya tulasī raghunāthagāthā-
भाषानिबन्धमतिमञ्जुलमातनोति ॥७॥
bhāṣānibandhamatimañjulamātanoti. 7.

Trans:

In accord with the various Purānas, Vedas, Agamas (Tantras), and with what has been recorded in the Rāmāyana and elsewhere, I, Tulsīdās, for the delight of my own heart, have composed these verses of the exquisite saga of Raghunāth in the common parlance.

सोरठा-*sorațhā:*

जो सुमिरत सिधि होइ गन नायक करिबर बदन ।
jo sumirata sidhi hoi gana nāyaka karibara badana,
करउ अनुग्रह सोइ बुद्धि रासि सुभ गुन सदन ॥१॥
karau anugraha soi buddhi rāsi subha guna sadana. 1.

Trans:

The mention of whose very name ensures success, who carries on his shoulders the head of beautiful elephant, who is a repository of wisdom and an abode of blessed qualities, may Ganesh, the leader of Shiva's retinue, shower his grace.

मूक होइ बाचाल पंगु चढइ गिरिबर गहन ।
mūka hoi bācāla paṁgu caḍhai giribara gahana,
जासु कृपाँ सो दयाल द्रवउ सकल कलि मल दहन ॥२॥
jāsu kṛpām̐ so dayāla dravau sakala kali mala dahana. 2.

Trans:

By whose favor the dumb become eloquent and the cripple ascend formidable mountains; He, who burns all the impurities of the Kali-Yug—may that merciful Harī, be moved to pity.

नील सरोरुह स्याम तरुन अरुन बारिज नयन ।
nīla saroruha syāma taruna aruna bārija nayana,
करउ सो मम उर धाम सदा छीरसागर सयन ॥३॥
karau so mama ura dhāma sadā chīrasāgara sayana. 3.

Trans:

O Harī, thou who ever slumbers on the milky ocean, thou whose body is dark as a blue lotus, thou with eyes lustrous as freshly bloomed red water-lilies—do take up thy abode in my heart as well.

कुंद इंदु सम देह उमा रमन करुना अयन ।
kuṁda iṁdu sama deha umā ramana karunā ayana,
जाहि दीन पर नेह करउ कृपा मर्दन मयन ॥४॥
jāhi dīna para neha karau kṛpā mardana mayana. 4.

Trans:

O Hara, Destroyer-of-Kāmdev, whose form resembles in color the jasmine flower and the moon, who is an abode of compassion, who is the refuge of the afflicted, O spouse of Umā, be thou gracious to me.

बंदउँ गुरु पद कंज कृपा सिंधु नररूप हरि ।
baṁdauṁ guru pada kaṁja kṛpā siṁdhu nararūpa hari,
महामोह तम पुंज जासु बचन रबि कर निकर ॥५॥
mahāmoha tama puṁja jāsu bacana rabi kara nikara. 5.
Trans:

I bow to the lotus feet of my Gurū, who is an ocean of mercy and is none other than Harī in human form, and whose words are a deluge of sunshine upon the darkness of Ignorance and Infatuation.

[Below are the ending verses of Tulsi Rāmāyana]
दोहा-*dohā:*

मो सम दीन न दीन हित तुम्ह समान रघुबीर ।
mo sama dīna na dīna hita tumha samāna raghubīra,
अस बिचारि रघुबंस मनि हरहु बिषम भव भीर ॥१३०क॥
asa bicāri raghubaṁsa mani harahu biṣama bhava bhīra. 130(ka).
कामिहि नारि पिआरि जिमि लोभिहि प्रिय जिमि दाम ।
kāmihi nāri piāri jimi lobhihi priya jimi dāma,
तिमि रघुनाथ निरंतर प्रिय लागहु मोहि राम ॥१३०ख॥
timi raghunātha niraṁtara priya lāgahu mohi rāma. 130(kha).
Trans:

There is no one as pathetic as I am and no one as gracious to the piteous as you, O Raghubīr: remember this, O glory of the race of Raghu, and rid me of the grievous burden of existence. As an amorous person is infatuated over their lover, and just as a greedy miser hankers after money, so for ever and ever, may you be always dear to me, O Rāma.

श्लोक-*śloka:*

यत्पूर्वं प्रभुणा कृतं सुकविना श्रीशम्भुना दुर्गमं
yatpūrvaṁ prabhuṇā kṛtaṁ sukavinā śrīśambhunā durgamaṁ
श्रीमद्रामपदाब्जभक्तिमनिशं प्राप्त्यै तु रामायणम् ।
śrīmadrāmapadābjabhaktimaniśaṁ prāptyai tu rāmāyaṇam,
मत्वा तद्रघुनाथमनिरतं स्वान्तस्तमःशान्तये
matvā tadraghunāthamaniratam svāntastamaḥśāntaye
भाषाबद्धमिदं चकार तुलसीदासस्तथा मानसम् ॥१॥
bhāṣābaddhamidaṁ cakāra tulasīdāsastathā mānasam. 1.
Trans:

The same esoteric Mānas-Rāmāyana, the Holy Lake of enactments of Shrī Rāma, that was brought to fore, in days of yore, by the blessed Shambhu, the foremost amongst poets—with the object of developing unceasing devotion to the beautiful lotus-feet of our beloved Lord: the all-merciful Rāma—has been likewise rendered into the common lingo by Tulsīdās for dispersing the gloom of his own soul, which it does—rife as it is with the name Rāma that alone gives this work a substance.

पुण्यं पापहरं सदा शिवकरं विज्ञानभक्तिप्रदं
puṇyaṁ pāpaharaṁ sadā śivakaraṁ vijñānabhaktipradaṁ
मायामोहमलापहं सुविमलं प्रेमाम्बुपूरं शुभम् ।
māyāmohamalāpahaṁ suvimalaṁ premāmbupūraṁ śubham,
श्रीमद्रामचरित्रमानसमिदं भक्त्यावगाहन्ति ये
śrīmadrāmacaritramānasamidaṁ bhaktyāvagāhanti ye
ते संसारपतङ्गघोरकिरणैर्दह्यन्ति नो मानवाः ॥२॥
te saṁsārapataṅgaghorakiraṇairdahyanti no mānavāḥ. 2.
Trans:

This glorious, purifying, blessed most limpid holy Mānas Lake of Shrī Rāma's enactments ever begets happiness. Verily, it bestows both Wisdom and Devotion; and it washes away delusion, infatuation and impurity; and brimful with a stream of love it inundates one with bliss supreme. Never scorched by the burning rays of the sun of worldly illusions are those who take a plunge in this most Holy-Lake of the Glories of Shrī Rāma.

सीताराम सीताराम सीताराम सीताराम सीताराम सीताराम सीताराम सीताराम सीताराम सीताराम सीताराम सीताराम सीताराम सीताराम सीताराम सीताराम सीताराम सीताराम सीताराम सीताराम
सीताराम सीताराम सीताराम सीताराम सीताराम सीताराम सीताराम सीताराम सीताराम सीताराम सीताराम सीताराम सीताराम सीताराम सीताराम सीताराम सीताराम सीताराम सीताराम सीताराम
सीताराम सीताराम सीताराम सीताराम सीताराम सीताराम सीताराम सीताराम सीताराम सीताराम सीताराम सीताराम सीताराम सीताराम सीताराम सीताराम सीताराम सीताराम सीताराम सीताराम
सीताराम सीताराम सीताराम सीताराम सीताराम सीताराम सीताराम सीताराम सीताराम सीताराम सीताराम सीताराम सीताराम सीताराम सीताराम सीताराम सीताराम सीताराम सीताराम सीताराम
सीताराम सीताराम सीताराम सीताराम सीताराम सीताराम सीताराम सीताराम सीताराम सीताराम सीताराम सीताराम सीताराम सीताराम सीताराम सीताराम सीताराम सीताराम सीताराम सीताराम
सीताराम सीताराम सीताराम सीताराम सीताराम सीताराम सीताराम सीताराम सीताराम सीताराम सीताराम सीताराम सीताराम सीताराम सीताराम सीताराम सीताराम सीताराम सीताराम सीताराम
सीताराम सीताराम सीताराम सीताराम सीताराम सीताराम सीताराम सीताराम सीताराम सीताराम सीताराम सीताराम सीताराम सीताराम सीताराम सीताराम सीताराम सीताराम सीताराम सीताराम

Below is reproduced from **Bhagavada Gītā, the Holy Book of Hindus, by Sushma.**
ISBNs: **978-1-945739-39-2** (Journal format) / **978-1-945739-36-1** (Paperback)/ **978-1-945739-37-8** (Hardback)

(Excerpts shown below are in reduced font-size)

— ॐ —

न त्वेवाहं जातु नासं न त्वं नेमे जनाधिपाः ।
na tvevāhaṁ jātu nāsaṁ na tvaṁ neme janādhipāḥ
न चैव न भविष्यामः सर्वे वयमतः परम् ॥२-१२॥
na caiva na bhaviṣyāmaḥ sarve vayamataḥ param (2-12)

There never was a time indeed when I—or you or any of these kings—did not exist; nor it is that hereafter any of us shall cease to be.

— ॐ —

देहिनोऽस्मिन्यथा देहे कौमारं यौवनं जरा ।
dehino'sminyathā dehe kaumāraṁ yauvanaṁ jarā
तथा देहान्तरप्राप्तिर्धीरस्तत्र न मुह्यति ॥२-१३॥
tathā dehāntaraprāptirdhīrastatra na muhyati (2-13)

Even as the embodied soul attains in this body the states of childhood, youth and old age—even so it obtains another body upon death; the wise do not get deluded witnessing such changes.

— ॐ —

मात्रास्पर्शास्तु कौन्तेय शीतोष्णसुखदुःखदाः ।
mātrāsparśāstu kaunteya śītoṣṇasukhaduḥkhadāḥ
आगमापायिनोऽनित्यास्तांस्तितिक्षस्व भारत ॥२-१४॥
āgamāpāyino'nityāstāṁstitikṣasva bhārata (2-14)

From the contact of the sense-organs with sense-objects, there arise heat and cold, and even so pleasures and pains; but these are all transitory and fleeting and are subject to coming and going—so therefore just endure them, O Bhārata.

— ॐ —

नासतो विद्यते भावो नाभावो विद्यते सतः ।
nāsato vidyate bhāvo nābhāvo vidyate sataḥ
उभयोरपि दृष्टोऽन्तस्त्वनयोस्तत्त्वदर्शिभिः ॥२-१६॥
ubhayorapi dṛṣṭo'ntastvanayostattvadarśibhiḥ (2-16)

The unreal has no existence, and the real never ceases to be—the conclusion of both is clearly

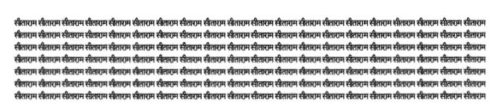

perceived to its stark reality by the knowers of Truth.

— ॐ —

अविनाशि तु तद्विद्धि येन सर्वमिदं ततम् ।
avināśi tu tadviddhi yena sarvamidaṁ tatam
विनाशमव्ययस्यास्य न कश्चित्कर्तुमर्हति ॥२-१७॥
vināśamavyayasyāsya na kaścitkartumarhati (2-17)

That One—by which this entire universe is pervaded—know That to be imperishable; verily no one can bring about the destruction of that Immutable Principle.

— ॐ —

य एनं वेत्ति हन्तारं यश्चैनं मन्यते हतम् ।
ya enaṁ vetti hantāraṁ yaścainaṁ manyate hatam
उभौ तौ न विजानीतो नायं हन्ति न हन्यते ॥२-१९॥
ubhau tau na vijānīto nāyaṁ hanti na hanyate (2-19)

He who thinks of It to be a slayer, and who thinks of It as slain, both of them are ignorant—for verily the Self neither kills, nor gets killed.

— ॐ —

नैनं छिन्दन्ति शस्त्राणि नैनं दहति पावकः ।
nainaṁ chindanti śastrāṇi nainaṁ dahati pāvakaḥ
न चैनं क्लेदयन्त्यापो न शोषयति मारुतः ॥२-२३॥
na cainaṁ kledayantyāpo na śoṣayati mārutaḥ (2-23)

Weapons do not cut the Self; and fires burn It not; and water cannot drench It; nor can It the winds dry.

— ॐ —

न जायते म्रियते वा कदाचिन् नायं भूत्वा भविता वा न भूयः ।
na jāyate mriyate vā kadācin nāyaṁ bhūtvā bhavitā vā na bhūyaḥ
अजो नित्यः शाश्वतोऽयं पुराणो न हन्यते हन्यमाने शरीरे ॥२-२०॥
ajo nityaḥ śāśvato'yaṁ purāṇo na hanyate hanyamāne śarīre (2-20)

The Self is never born, nor does it ever die; nor does it come into existence by the body coming into being. Verily the Soul is unborn, immutable, constant, eternal and ancient-most. Even though the body is slain, the indwelling Self always persists unslain.

— ॐ —

वासांसि जीर्णानि यथा विहाय नवानि गृह्णाति नरोऽपराणि ।
vāsāṁsi jīrṇāni yathā vihāya navāni gṛhṇāti naro'parāṇi
तथा शरीराणि विहाय जीर्णान्यन्यानि संयाति नवानि देही ॥२-२२॥
tathā śarīrāṇi vihāya jīrṇānyanyāni saṁyāti navāni dehī (2-22)

Discarding worn-out garments, just as a person puts on new garbs, in like fashion does the embodied Self—casting off outworn bodies—enters into other newer ones.

— ॐ —

अव्यक्तादीनि भूतानि व्यक्तमध्यानि भारत ।
avyaktādīni bhūtāni vyaktamadhyāni bhārata

अव्यक्तनिधनान्येव तत्र का परिदेवना ॥२-२८॥
avyaktanidhanānyeva tatra kā paridevanā (2-28)

Beings have the Unmanifest as their beginning; and upon death they return to that Unmanifest again. Between birth and death—only during the interim—do the beings become manifest; so wherefore lament for them, O Bhārata?

— ॐ —

देही नित्यमवध्योऽयं देहे सर्वस्य भारत ।
dehī nityamavadhyo'yaṁ dehe sarvasya bhārata
तस्मात्सर्वाणि भूतानि न त्वं शोचितुमर्हसि ॥२-३०॥
tasmātsarvāṇi bhūtāni na tvaṁ śocitumarhasi (2-30)

The indwelling Self, within the bodies of all, is eternally indestructible, O Bhārata; therefore, you ought not to grieve for any being.

— ॐ —

यावानर्थ उदपाने सर्वतः सम्प्लुतोदके ।
yāvānartha udapāne sarvataḥ samplutodake
तावान्सर्वेषु वेदेषु ब्राह्मणस्य विजानतः ॥२-४६॥
tāvānsarveṣu vedeṣu brāhmaṇasya vijānataḥ (2-46)

All the purposes which a small reservoir serves, is served entirely by a vast lake full of water. Likewise the purpose which all the Vedas serve, is already attained by one who is in complete knowledge of Brahama.

— ॐ —

योगस्थः कुरु कर्माणि सङ्गं त्यक्त्वा धनञ्जय ।
yogasthaḥ kuru karmāṇi saṅgaṁ tyaktvā dhanañjaya
सिद्ध्यसिद्ध्योः समो भूत्वा समत्वं योग उच्यते ॥२-४८॥
siddhyasiddhyoḥ samo bhūtvā samatvaṁ yoga ucyate (2-48)

Established in Yoga, perform Karma renouncing all attachments, O Dhananjaya, remaining unconcerned as to the outcome—be it failure or success; this equanimity of mind is what is called Karma-Yoga.

— ॐ —

कर्मजं बुद्धियुक्ता हि फलं त्यक्त्वा मनीषिणः ।
karmajaṁ buddhiyuktā hi phalaṁ tyaktvā manīṣiṇaḥ
जन्मबन्धविनिर्मुक्ताः पदं गच्छन्त्यनामयम् ॥२-५१॥
janmabandhavinirmuktāḥ padaṁ gacchantyanāmayam (2-51)

Endowed with wisdom, renouncing the fruits born of action, attaining self-realization, freed from the shackles of births and deaths—verily a Yogī enters that abode which is void of sorrows.

— ॐ —

यदा संहरते चायं कूर्मोऽङ्गानीव सर्वशः ।
yadā saṁharate cāyaṁ kūrmo'ṅgānīva sarvaśaḥ
इन्द्रियाणीन्द्रियार्थेभ्यस्तस्य प्रज्ञा प्रतिष्ठिता ॥२-५८॥
indriyāṇīndriyārthebhyastasya prajñā pratiṣṭhitā (2-58)

When one can altogether withdraw the senses from the sense-objects—even as a tortoise its limbs—then his wisdom is said to be steady.

— ॐ —

विषया विनिवर्तन्ते निराहारस्य देहिनः ।
viṣayā vinivartante nirāhārasya dehinaḥ
रसवर्जं रसोऽप्यस्य परं दृष्ट्वा निवर्तते ॥२-५९॥
rasavarjaṁ raso'pyasya paraṁ dṛṣṭvā nivartate (2-59)

Sense enjoyments can be restricted through physical restraint by an abstemious being, but a relish for them may still persist; even this relish ceases when the highest bliss of the Supreme is realized.

— ॐ —

कर्मेन्द्रियाणि संयम्य य आस्ते मनसा स्मरन् ।
karmendriyāṇi saṁyamya ya āste manasā smaran
इन्द्रियार्थान्विमूढात्मा मिथ्याचारः स उच्यते ॥३-६॥
indriyārthānvimūḍhātmā mithyācāraḥ sa ucyate (3-6)

The fool who outwardly restraining the organs of action sits dwelling upon the senses-objects through the mind—that man of deluded intellect is called a hypocrite.

— ॐ —

यस्त्विन्द्रियाणि मनसा नियम्यारभतेऽर्जुन ।
yastvindriyāṇi manasā niyamyārabhate'rjuna
कर्मेन्द्रियैः कर्मयोगमसक्तः स विशिष्यते ॥३-७॥
karmendriyaiḥ karmayogamasaktaḥ sa viśiṣyate (3-7)

But he who controls the sense-organs through the mind—performing Karma-Yoga through the organs of actions while remaining unattached—that wise one excels, O Arjuna.

सीताराम सीताराम सीताराम सीताराम सीताराम सीताराम सीताराम सीताराम सीताराम सीताराम सीताराम सीताराम सीताराम सीताराम सीताराम सीताराम सीताराम सीताराम सीताराम सीताराम
सीताराम सीताराम सीताराम सीताराम सीताराम सीताराम सीताराम सीताराम सीताराम सीताराम सीताराम सीताराम सीताराम सीताराम सीताराम सीताराम सीताराम सीताराम सीताराम सीताराम
सीताराम सीताराम सीताराम सीताराम सीताराम सीताराम सीताराम सीताराम सीताराम सीताराम सीताराम सीताराम सीताराम सीताराम सीताराम सीताराम सीताराम सीताराम सीताराम सीताराम
सीताराम सीताराम सीताराम सीताराम सीताराम सीताराम सीताराम सीताराम सीताराम सीताराम सीताराम सीताराम सीताराम सीताराम सीताराम सीताराम सीताराम सीताराम सीताराम सीताराम
सीताराम सीताराम सीताराम सीताराम सीताराम सीताराम सीताराम सीताराम सीताराम सीताराम सीताराम सीताराम सीताराम सीताराम सीताराम सीताराम सीताराम सीताराम सीताराम सीताराम
सीताराम सीताराम सीताराम सीताराम सीताराम सीताराम सीताराम सीताराम सीताराम सीताराम सीताराम सीताराम सीताराम सीताराम सीताराम सीताराम सीताराम सीताराम सीताराम सीताराम
सीताराम सीताराम सीताराम सीताराम सीताराम सीताराम सीताराम सीताराम सीताराम सीताराम सीताराम सीताराम सीताराम सीताराम सीताराम सीताराम सीताराम सीताराम सीताराम सीताराम

Below is reproduced from **Ashtavakra Gita, A Fiery Octave in Ascension, by Vidya Wati.**
ISBNs: **978-1-945739-42-2** (Journal format) / **978-1-945739-46-0** (Paperback) / **978-1-945739-48-4** (Pocket-sized) / **978-1-945739-47-7** (Hardback)

(Excerpts shown below are in reduced font-size)

— ॐ —

अहं कर्तेत्यहंमानमहाकृष्णाहिदंशितः ।
ahaṁ kartetyahaṁmānamahākṛṣṇāhidaṁśitaḥ ,
नाहं कर्तेति विश्वासामृतं पीत्वा सुखी भव ॥१-८॥
nāhaṁ karteti viśvāsāmṛtaṁ pītvā sukhī bhava (1-8)

— ॐ —

May thou
—who have been bitten by the deadly serpent of egoism,
who persist delirious in its venom,
hallucinating, “I am the Doer”—
drink of the antidote of faith
—partake of the curative reality—
which avers: "I am not the Doer";
and replete with that nectar,
may thou abide ever glad.

— ॐ —

एको विशुद्धबोधोऽहमिति निश्चयवह्निना ।
eko viśuddhabodho'hamiti niścayavahninā ,
प्रज्वाल्याज्ञानगहनं वीतशोकः सुखी भव ॥१-९॥
prajvālyājñānagahanaṁ vītaśokaḥ sukhī bhava (1-9)

— ॐ —

Burn down this wilderness of Ignorance in the Fiery Knowledge-of-the-Self,
the essence of which Truth is the firm conviction that proclaims,
“I am the One Reality,
the all-pervading pristine Consciousness”;
and thus freed of pain grief sorrows,
may thou abide in supreme happiness.

— ॐ —

कूटस्थं बोधमद्वैतमात्मानं परिभावय ।
kūṭasthaṁ bodhamadvaitamātmānaṁ paribhāvaya ,
आभासोऽहं भ्रमं मुक्त्वा भावं बाह्यमथान्तरम् ॥१-१३॥
ābhāso'haṁ bhramaṁ muktvā
bhāvaṁ bāhyamathāntaram (1-13)

— ॐ —

Giving up the mistaken identification with the body, the external crust;
and rid also of identifying yourself
as being the ego and mind
—the superimposed delusions which are but reflections of the Ātmā—
meditate on yourself as being none of these but purely the Ātmā:
Immutable Consciousness,
the One without a second.

— ॐ —

यथा न तोयतो भिन्नास्तरङ्गाः फेनबुद्बुदाः ।
yathā na toyato bhinnāstaraṅgāḥ phenabudbudāḥ ,
आत्मनो न तथा भिन्नं विश्वमात्मविनिर्गतम् ॥२-४॥
ātmano na tathā bhinnaṁ viśvamātmavinirgatam (2-4)

— ॐ —

Just as
the waves foam and bubbles
are identical to the water of which they are made,
even so
this seemingly real universe
has emanated from the Param-Ātmā,
and is none other than the Ātmā
—my Self.

— ॐ —

प्रकाशो मे निजं रूपं नातिरिक्तोऽस्म्यहं ततः ।
prakāśo me nijaṁ rūpaṁ nātirikto'smyahaṁ tataḥ ,
यदा प्रकाशते विश्वं तदाहं भास एव हि ॥२-८॥
yadā prakāśate viśvaṁ tadāhaṁ bhāsa eva hi (2-8)

— ॐ —

My innate essence is a Fiery Light—
and other than the effulgence of Consciousness
I am nothing else.
When the universe shines forth,
it does so borrowing the glow of my brilliance.
Through and through everything which is manifest anywhere,
there is nothing except for the Fiery Ātmā
shining all splendorous.

— ॐ —

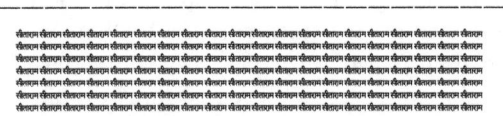

मत्तो विनिर्गतं विश्वं मय्येव लयमेष्यति ।
matto vinirgataṁ viśvaṁ mayyeva layameṣyati ,
मृदि कुम्भो जले वीचिः कनके कटकं यथा ॥२-१०॥
mṛdi kumbho jale vīciḥ kanake kaṭakaṁ yathā (2-10)

All this here, emerges out of me;
it exists in me;
and within me again it becomes dissolved
—like an earthen jar returning to its component clay,
...or a wave
blending back into the water again,
...or a gold bracelet
melting into the pureness of its element
—having become bereft of form
bereft of name.

द्वैतमूलमहो दुःखं नान्यत्तस्याऽस्ति भेषजम् ।
dvaitamūlamaho duḥkhaṁ nānyattasyā'sti bheṣajam ,
दृश्यमेतन् मृषा सर्वमेकोऽहं चिद्रसोमलः ॥२-१६॥
dṛśyametan mṛṣā sarvameko'haṁ cidrasomalaḥ (2-16)

The notion of duality
is at the root of all grief and misery.
There is no other cure for sorrow
except the realization of the Truth, that
"There are no two here—it is all just One."

All this perceived multifariousness
is just an apparition,
and behind it all is just the One pristine Reality void of defilements,
comprised in bliss and consciousness.

नाहं देहो न मे देहो जीवो नाहमहं हि चित् ।
nāhaṁ deho na me deho jīvo nāhamahaṁ hi cit ,
अयमेव हि मे बन्ध आसीद्या जीविते स्पृहा ॥२-२२॥
ayameva hi me bandha āsīdyā jīvite spṛhā (2-22)

I am not this body
—and nor had I ever a body—
I am not the Jīva,
I am nothing but a Pure Consciousness.
This indeed was my bondage:
that I once had this 'me' and 'mine';
and that I thirsted for life
in greed, desires, covetousness;
and that I fancied little bites of joys
—while in fact
the entire ocean of bliss was just I myself.

यत् पदं प्रेप्सवो दीनाः शक्राद्याः सर्वदेवताः ।
yat padaṁ prepsavo dīnāḥ śakrādyāḥ sarvadevatāḥ ,
अहो तत्र स्थितो योगी न हर्षमुपगच्छति ॥४-२॥
aho tatra sthito yogī na harṣamupagacchati (4-2)

Even suffering the state of mirthful revelries
—those ravishing spheres of pleasures which even gods like Indra yearn for disconsolately—
the yogi finds no excitement existing in them
—being that he always abides
in That-Ocean-of-Bliss
where such morsels of delights
are but tiny fleeting waves
...flapping away

न ते सङ्गोऽस्ति केनापि किं शुद्धस्त्यक्तुमिच्छसि ।
na te saṅgo'sti kenāpi kiṁ śuddhastyaktumicchasi ,
सङ्घातविलयं कुर्वन्नेवमेव लयं व्रज ॥५-१॥
saṅghātavilayaṁ kurvannevameva layaṁ vraja (5-1)

There is nothing at all here attached to which you lie bound in fetters.
Pure and taintless you already are—
so what is that you must needs give up?

Renounce simply the idea of a body—
set aside this composite organism to rest.
Give up identifying yourself with this assemblage of skin, bone, organs.
Abide Dissolved,
knowing that you are not anything material
but the Ātmā pure.

यस्य बोधोदये तावत्स्वप्नवद् भवति भ्रमः ।
yasya bodhodaye tāvatsvapnavad bhavati bhramaḥ ,
तस्मै सुखैकरूपाय नमः शान्ताय तेजसे ॥१८-१॥
tasmai sukhaikarūpāya namaḥ śāntāya tejase (18-1)

Salutation to that Fiery Light—
self-effulgent, self-existent, independent,
which is pristine consciousness
which is tranquility,
which is bliss,
which is abiding existence—
in whose dawn,
this dark delusive universe
—which has you enslaved—
vanishes away
like the dream of a dark night.

व्यामोहमात्रविरतौ स्वरूपादानमात्रतः ।
vyāmohamātraviratau svarūpādānamātrataḥ ,
वीतशोका विराजन्ते निरावरणदृष्टयः ॥१८-६॥
vītaśokā virājante nirāvaraṇadṛṣṭayaḥ (18-6)

With their delusions dispelled,
those who abide cognized of the Self
—the fiery glow of pure consciousness shining within—
their distress is now at end;
and they live free of sorrows
—in a completeness of Bliss.

क्व विक्षेपः क्व चैकाग्र्यं क्व निर्बोधः क्व मूढता ।
kva vikṣepaḥ kva caikāgryaṁ kva nirbodhaḥ kva mūḍhatā ,
क्व हर्षः क्व विषादो वा सर्वदा निष्क्रियस्य मे ॥२०-९॥
kva harṣaḥ kva viṣādo vā sarvadā niṣkriyasya me (20-9)

Whither went concentration?

...and what happened to all those distractions?
...whither the deluded soul?
...and whither the burdensome bag of delusions?
...where went charms and delights of the world?
...and where went sorrows?
For me, it has all coalesced into a oneness.
Bereft of any karmas,
I am just the Ātmā now.

सीताराम सीताराम सीताराम सीताराम सीताराम सीताराम सीताराम सीताराम सीताराम सीताराम सीताराम सीताराम सीताराम सीताराम सीताराम सीताराम सीताराम सीताराम सीताराम सीताराम
सीताराम सीताराम सीताराम सीताराम सीताराम सीताराम सीताराम सीताराम सीताराम सीताराम सीताराम सीताराम सीताराम सीताराम सीताराम सीताराम सीताराम सीताराम सीताराम सीताराम
सीताराम सीताराम सीताराम सीताराम सीताराम सीताराम सीताराम सीताराम सीताराम सीताराम सीताराम सीताराम सीताराम सीताराम सीताराम सीताराम सीताराम सीताराम सीताराम सीताराम
सीताराम सीताराम सीताराम सीताराम सीताराम सीताराम सीताराम सीताराम सीताराम सीताराम सीताराम सीताराम सीताराम सीताराम सीताराम सीताराम सीताराम सीताराम सीताराम सीताराम
सीताराम सीताराम सीताराम सीताराम सीताराम सीताराम सीताराम सीताराम सीताराम सीताराम सीताराम सीताराम सीताराम सीताराम सीताराम सीताराम सीताराम सीताराम सीताराम सीताराम
सीताराम सीताराम सीताराम सीताराम सीताराम सीताराम सीताराम सीताराम सीताराम सीताराम सीताराम सीताराम सीताराम सीताराम सीताराम सीताराम सीताराम सीताराम सीताराम सीताराम
सीताराम सीताराम सीताराम सीताराम सीताराम सीताराम सीताराम सीताराम सीताराम सीताराम सीताराम सीताराम सीताराम सीताराम सीताराम सीताराम सीताराम सीताराम सीताराम सीताराम

Below is reproduced from **Vivekachūḍāmani of Shankaracharya, the Fiery Crest-Jewel of Wisdom, by Vidya Wati.** ISBNs: **978-1-945739-41-5** (Journal format) / **978-1-945739-44-6**(Paperback) / **978-1-945739-79-8**(Pocket-sized) / **978-1-945739-45-3**(Hardback)

(Excerpts shown below are in reduced font-size)

लब्ध्वा कथञ्चिन्नरजन्म दुर्लभं तत्रापि पुंस्त्वं श्रुतिपारदर्शनम् ।
labdhvā kathañcinnarajanma durlabhaṁ tatrāpi puṁstvaṁ śrutipāradarśanam ,
यस्त्वात्ममुक्तौ न यतेत मूढधीः स ह्यात्महा स्वं विनिहन्त्यसद्ग्रहात् ॥४॥
yastvātmamuktau na yateta mūḍhadhīḥ sa hyātmahā svaṁ vinihantyasadgrahāt (4)

He who, having by some means obtained this privileged human birth born a man—and furthermore having knowledge and learning and grasp of the sacred scriptures—does not exert himself for self-liberation, that fool is certainly committing suicide thereby—for he imperils himself by holding as life-support those very things which themselves are tenuous and unreal.

ब्रह्म सत्यं जगन्मिथ्येत्येवंरूपो विनिश्चयः ।
brahma satyaṁ jaganmithyetyevaṁrūpo viniścayaḥ ,
सोऽयं नित्यानित्यवस्तुविवेकः समुदाहृतः ॥२०॥
so'yaṁ nityānityavastuvivekaḥ samudāhṛtaḥ (20)

"*Brahama* alone is Real (self-existent), and the universe non-Real (not self-existent)"—the insight, discernment, and firm conviction by which one comprehends this Vedic dictum: that is designated to be *Viveka* (or Discrimination between the Real and the non-Real).

अहङ्कारादिदेहान्तान् बन्धानज्ञानकल्पितान् ।
ahaṅkārādidehāntān bandhānajñānakalpitān ,
स्वस्वरूपावबोधेन मोक्तुमिच्छा मुमुक्षुता ॥२७॥
svasvarūpāvabodhena moktumicchā mumukṣutā (27)

An intense yearning for Freedom—to be released of all bondages, from that of egoism to that of body, to be relieved of all thralldoms superimposed by dint of Ignorance—by realizing one's Real Nature: that is designated to be *Mumukshutā* (or Longing for Liberation).

मोक्षकारणसामग्र्यां भक्तिरेव गरीयसी ।
mokṣakāraṇasāmagryāṁ bhaktireva garīyasī ,
स्वस्वरूपानुसन्धानं भक्तिरित्यभिधीयते ॥३१॥
svasvarūpānusandhānaṁ bhaktirityabhidhīyate (31)

Among the means most conducive to Liberation, *Bhaktī* holds a supreme spot. A constant contemplation and seeking of one's true Self, one's Real Nature—that is designated to be *Bhaktī* (Devotion).

ऋणमोचनकर्तारः पितुः सन्ति सुतादयः ।
ṛṇamocanakartāraḥ pituḥ santi sutādayaḥ ,
बन्धमोचनकर्ता तु स्वस्मादन्यो न कश्चन ॥५१॥
bandhamocanakartā tu svasmādanyo na kaścana (51)

A father may have his sons and others to redeem him from his financial debts, but there is no one other than one's own Self to deliver one from the within bondages that are upon the Self (and which are self-imposed).

तस्मात्सर्वप्रयत्नेन भवबन्धविमुक्तये ।
tasmātsarvaprayatnena bhavabandhavimuktaye ,
स्वैरेव यत्नः कर्तव्यो रोगादाविव पण्डितैः ॥६६॥
svaireva yatnaḥ kartavyo rogādāviva paṇḍitaiḥ (66)

Therefore—just as in the case of bodily diseases and internal maladies—the wise should strive personally and with every means in his power, to free himself from the bondages of this dreadful transmigratory disease of repeated births and deaths.

मा भैष्ट विद्वंस्तव नास्त्यपायः संसारसिन्धोस्तरणेऽस्त्युपायः ।
mā bhaiṣṭa vidvaṁstava nāstyapāyaḥ saṁsārasindhostaraṇe'styupāyaḥ ,
येनैव याता यतयोऽस्य पारं तमेव मार्गं तव निर्दिशामि ॥४३॥
yenaiva yātā yatayo'sya pāraṁ tameva mārgaṁ tava nirdiśāmi (43)

Fear not, O learned one, there is no death for thee; verily there is a sovereign means of crossing this sea of relative existence. That very supreme path, treading which our ancient sages of yore have managed to go beyond—that very way I shall now inculcate to thee.

www.ingramcontent.com/pod-product-compliance
Lightning Source LLC
Chambersburg PA
CBHW060504240426
43661CB00007B/912
* 9 7 8 1 9 4 5 7 3 9 9 1 0 *